GLOBALIZATION AND PLANTATION WORKERS IN NORTH-EAST INDIA

GLOBALIZATION AND PLANTATION WORKERS IN NORTH-EAST INDIA

K.R. Sharma, T.C. Das

PUBLICATIONS
KALPAZ PUBLICATIONS
DELHI-110052

Globalization and Plantation Workers in North-East India

Rs. 690

ISBN: 81-7835-713-5

Published in 2009 in India by
Kalpaz Publications
C-30, Satyawati Nagar,
Delhi-110052
E-mail: kalpaz@hotmail.com
Phone : 9212729499

Laser Type Setting by: Quick Media, Delhi
Printed at : G. Print Process, Delhi

Dedicated to

Central Board for Workers Education, Ministry of Labour
and
Employment, Government of India, Nagpur, India

CONTENTS

List of Tables

Preface

Globalization and Plantation Workers in North-East India deals with the emerging challenges for the plantation workers of North-East India during the last two decades of the implementation of Liberalization, Privatization and Globalization policy of Indian government in various industries of the country. The plantation workers are of mainly unskilled agrarian type since the plantation industry itself is mainly agrarian in nature. The issue like globalization appears to be of secondary importance in so far as their socio-economic development is concerned. The pertinent question explored in the study is both the positive and negative impacts of the globalization among the workers. Looking into this, the impacts of globalization has been viewed from the prospective of a case study relating to the Darjeeling tea industry which concerns much to the Tea Board of India and therefore the Government of India. The globalization is a challenge for the stack holders of Darjeeling tea industry having proclamation of International Geographical Indication certificate from the global tea buyers. This may be the reason why Darjeeling tea is the matter of great concern for all of them today in the age of globalization. Coming to the question of socio-economic development of the workers, it is explored from the study that plantation workers are however have been under marginalisation, informalization and feminization processes during the last two decades of globalization.

Tea industry of North-East India contributes more than two thousand crores of rupees to the national eschequor. Whatever efforts are being made to the revival of tea industry in the region from the various corners of the society, they have prioritize the social clause paradigms for the plantation workers who are marginalized in so far as the industrialism in true sense of the term is concerned. This may be the reason why almost 71.0% of plantation workers are females in Darjeeling tea industry today and there is every possibility to reach the trend to 95.0% by 2020 A.D. It is because of the fact that male folks of the plantation industry are galloping away the plantations for non-plantation jobs in the country or aborad. This has enabled the tea garden management to introduce pro-rata system in each and every aspect of the plantation system especially in regard to welfare incentives of the workers. The pro-rata system as a new of form of structural adjustment policy as being brought about by the globalization appears to have been unilaterally implemented without any utter objection from trade unions and government of the country. In this comprehensive study, we have incorporated the various facets of plantation industry, challenges and prospects of the industry in near future. In regard to the marginalized plantation workers, their socio-economic, cultural, health and ethinicity aspects have been the main focus of the study especially ever since the introduction of Liberalisation, Privatisation and Globalization policy in the country.

The work would not have been possible unless we get the cooperation from our family members, friends, management and workers of Darjeeling tea industry. So, we are thankful to them all. We are also grateful to the authorities of Central Board for Workers Education, Ministry of Labour and Employment, Government of India, Nagpur for their moral supports.

Finally, we are also thankful to Shri Amit Garg, the Director, Publications of the Kalpaz Publications, New Delhi for taking keen interest to publish the book.

Siliguri: 29.5.2008 **Dr. K.R. Sharma,**
Shri T.C. Das

1

Introduction

First Decade of Globalization and Plantation Industry in India

Background

With the Globalization of Indian economy, the tea industry has been passing through a tough time to exist and compete the other tea growing countries of the world. Considering the changes occurring at the national level as well as to introduce the readers with the ideas about the present phase of globalization, its impacts among the workers and future prospect of tea industry, the present work has been done. In the present section of the study, we shall see the background of tea industry, problems emerged and how the crisis started during the first decade of globalization. The established tea industry of the country had to face severe problems due to the emergence of small growers of tea in so far as the development prospect of the same in the country during nineties of the 19th century was concerned. This along with the introduction of new plantations in tea growing zones of the country had also encouraged to sprout new and new problems in the plantation frontiers. Further, with the emergence of plantations in other countries of the world, the structure of competition became more and more herculean in terms of cost effectiveness (Asopa: 2004) and quality aspects of the plantation products. So, in order to understand the impacts of globalization among the plantation workers, let us first understand its background in the national perspective.

Evolution of Tea Industry in India

It is believed that long back in 1831 tea bush was discovered in Assam where its tea plantations were started and gradually spread over the whole of North-East India (Bhadra: 1997). In the process, the first tea plantation was started on an experimental basis in 1833 by the colonial government in Chabua (Diburgarh district of Assam). Interestingly, the expansion of the government owned tea plantations could not persist long and therefore private tea enterprenurs were encouraged from 1859 and subsequently the private enterprenurs could expand and develop the tea plantations successfully. By 1850, the exact acarage under tea came to 1,876 hectares in Assam. The area increased to 7,599 in 1859 and 25,174 hectares in 1859. It further increased to 56,000 hectares in 1876. It was therefore observed that by the end of 1870-71, about 7 million acres of land were brought under the tea plantations though the accurate area was of merely 8.0% of the total land owned by the plantations. The decade from 1901 to 1911 witnessed a slow growth of tea plantations. For first time in 1838, eight chests of made tea was sent to London Auction Centre. In 1947, only 30.0% of 1.5 million acres of land under plantations was occupied by tea planters in Assam. However, after 1870, the tea gardens were expanded intensively in the state of Assam.

Tripura was the first state of North-East India after Assam to introduce tea plantation industry. The recommendation of young scientist named A.C. Bhattacharjee helped to cultivate tea in Tripura, being enthusiased by the then Raja of Tripura, Birendra Kishore Manikya who introduced "Tashkhidri Taluk" system in Tripura. In Tripura, first tea garden was started in 1916. This was the crucial period for tea industry in India due to recession of tea. But after 1922, the recession was subsided which invariably encouraged tea planters to cultivate about 8,386 acres of land under tea. The basic difference between Assam and Tripura plantations was that in case of former state, mostly the tea gardens were under the British planters while in Tripura, all tea gardens were of Indian origins.

The introduction of tea industry in Dooars area of West Bengal was started with the introduction of Gajoldoba tea estate in 1874 by G.I. Gonnings (Mukherjee: 1997). Within the span of eight years, *i.e.*, from 1870 to 1878, thirteen tea estates were established in Dooars with 11,984 acres. The growth of tea industry in eighties was so rapid that the acarage under tea went up to six times from 1872 till 1892 (Griffith:1967). During the period commencing from 1901 to 1951, the area under tea doubled (Bhadra: 1997).

The history of introduction of tea industry in Darjeeling is associated with the posting of Dr. Campbell from Kathmandu to Darjeeling in 1840 (Das: 1947, Hunter: 1876). In 1834, the Governor-General of India, Lord William Bentick appointed a committee to find out the possibility of introducing tea industry in North-East India including the Darjeeling hills. The committee gave favourable report. This along with the initiative of Dr. Campbell, a tea plantation was started at Allobari (Darjeeling) on an experimental basis. The Allobari garden opened up the eye of the British planters to establish tea gardens like Ging, Ambotia, Tukdah, Phoobsering, Badamtam, Tukvar, Makaibari, Pandam and Stienthal in Darjeeling hills. The number of garden went on increasing (O' Malley: 1907). With the successful venture in the hills, the planters started exploring the Terai belt of Darjeeling district for the same end and in this pursuit, the first tea garden was started at New Chumpta in 1865. By 1866, thirty nine gardens were started with 10,000 acres of land. By 1874, the number of gardens reached to 113 with 18,888 acres of land (Das: 1947). Again, in 1885, the number of garden reached to 175 with 38,499 acres. After 1935, the number of tea gardens started decreasing considerably in Darjeeling hills.

Objectives of present section of the study

1. The prime objective of the present section of the study is to highlight the problems and prospects of tea industry in first decade of globalization.
2. To assess the importance of 11 lakhs tea plantation workers their future, various labour acts relating the plantation workers of the country, etc.
3. To understand the role of small grower tea sectors and new tea plantations in the national economy.
4. To understand the evolution and growth of tea industry in India.
5. To study research on Human Development aspect of tea industry.
6. To study the field practices and manufacture of tea.

Position of Tea Industry in Nineties

With the introduction of liberalization, privatization and globalization policy to Indian economy, tea frontiers started facing lot of problems including the stiff competition from other tea growing countries of the world like Srilanka, Kenya, Indonesia etc. Amidst the situation, what needed was to identify the basic strategies of the industry to make it more and more competitive and viable so that we could increase yield and production in every tea growing regions of the country. That could be visualised by identifying the new areas for the production of tea. Secondly, that was possible if thorough innovation and research were conducted in proceeding phases of globalization on the basis of the then position of tea industry in the country.

Number of Tea Estates

As per the figures of Tea Board of India, there were 13,936 tea gardens in India of which 2,948 tea estates were located in various states of North India and 10,988 tea estates in South India. One of the interesting development of tea industry in India was the growth of small tea growers.

Altogether, there were 654 such tea estates in North India and 240 in South India. Again, there were 7,000 to 20,000 small grower tea estates in Assam (Tea Board of India : 1996). However, that aspect will be discussed in detail later on in the next section of the study. Here, for the sake of analytical convenience, growth and development of tea industry during the first phase of globalization has been analysed comparatively with the past few decades.

Table 1. Tea Estates in India (1996)

Region	*1961*	*1971*	*1981*	*1991*	*1993*	*1995-1996*
Assam	744	750	777	848	851	850
West Bengal	301	296	305	347	347	347
North India	2421	2517	2563	2936	2949	2948
South India	6978	9498	10,843	10,937	10,969	10,988
Total India	9,399	12,015	13,412	13,873	13,918	13,936

Source: Consultative Committee of Plantation Associations: 1996, Calcutta.

The Table No. 1 indicates that the number of tea estates had been increasing in India from 9,399 in 1961 to 13,936 in 1995-1996. This shows that the tea industry appeared to have its bright future.

Area under Tea

There were 421913 hectares under tea in India of which 345,788 hectares were in North India while South India had 76,125 hectares. It would be more evident from the following Table No. 2.

Table 2. Area Under Tea (in Hectares)

Region	*1961*	*1971*	*1981*	*1991*	*1993*	*1995-1996*
Assam	162367	182325	203038	233284	231942	234580
West Bengal	82705	88499	93971	101922	100489	100650
North India	256928	282729	309066	345182	342789	345988
South India	74301	73787	74563	75288	75542	76125
All India	331229	356516	383629	420470	418331	421913

Source : Tea Digest: 1996

The Table No. 2 indicates that between 1961 and 1995-96, the area under tea had increased by 38,284 hectares and 1,126 hectares on the average per year. That was possible mainly due to the addition of area under tea. During 1981-1993, a total of 28,084 hectares in Assam, 6,518 hectares in West Bengal, 33,723 hectares in other states of North India, 1,015 hectares in South India and thus, 34,738 hectares were added at all India level.

Extension, Replacements and Replantings

At the national level, the history of tea bush was over one hundred and fifty years old. Hardly, the replacement and replanting of tea bush had been done. That caused for the low bush productivity of tea in India. This is evident from the following Table No. 3.

Table 3. Area under Extension, Replacement and Replanting (in Hectare)

Year	*Extension*	*Replacement*	*Replanting*
1961	1713.47	352.77	1781.87
1962	1852.20	393.18	1607.48
1963	2224.86	401.13	1571.16
1964	3135.38	411.62	1758.84
1965	3860.15	551.14	2024.26
1966	3494.43	510.45	1937.36
1967	3328.88	459.88	1628.07
1968	2960.81	474.63	1397.11
1969	2635.19	373.20	1188.68
1970	2174.68	277.98	987.42
1971	2355.35	201.12	1118.96
1972	1831.63	194.66	1322.21
1973	1632.98	180.36	1109.22
1974	1801.01	322.48	1090.35
1975	1762.29	319.83	1220.07

(Contd.)

Year	*Extension*	*Replacement*	*Replanting*
1976	1658.89	362.22	1117.83
1977	1769.69	366.26	1202.76
1978	2234.11	267.14	1225.25
1979	3464.55	399.22	1246.22
1980	3075.33	468.78	1023.79
1981	1986.50	475.75	1288.98
1982	1981.93	188.83	1355.55
1983	1945.89	210.52	1278.14
1984	2414.82	184.40	1225.77
1985	2390.35	296.73	1085.61
1986	3491.29	479.27	1259.46
1987	3070.50	476.73	1195.33
1988	2780.05	374.31	1303.88
1989	2558.29	381.65	1402.56
1990	2525.05	376.62	1394.61
1991	2423.05	434.90	1495.48
1992	2392.71	518.62	1282.15
1993	2462.53	450.47	1338.65

Source : Ibid., A, 4: CCPA Report : 1996.

The Table No. 3 of the study indicates that the average annual rate of tea under cultivation and therefore its extension was 2543.25 hectares. Similarly, it is also transparent from the table that on the average only 379.28 hectares of land had been brought under replacement of old tea bushes and finally, only 1389.53 hectares under the replanting scheme.

Tea Production Scenario during the Early Phase of Globalization

Ever since 1961, the highest production at 761 million kilograms was recorded in 1993 and thereafter the production is going down to 754 million kilograms in 1995 and in 1996 it was 780.34 million kilograms. However, on the whole 53.0% increase was achieved by increasing 9.0% area under tea. This will be very clear if we see the Table No. 4 of the study.

Table 4. Tea Production (in Thousand kg.)

State	*1984*	*1985*	*1986*	*1993*	*1994*	*1995*	*1996*
Assam	383533	352538	335492	410430	400732	339133	424864
West Bengal	148293	157371	141270	162669	158825	160305	165375
Total North India	491428	514295	4811299	581534	567955	567973	599626
Total South India	148436	141867	139504	179292	184940	185949	180408
Total India	639864	656162	620803	760826	752895	753922	780034

Source: Tea Digest : Tea Board of India : 1996; 7-8.

The Table No. 4 of the study shows that the acarage percentage of distribution between North and South India is 75.0% and 25.0% respectively. It means that 75.0% of total production is done in North India and only 25.0% in South India.

Tea Yield during the period

Despite of having mainfold, constraints, there were ample possibility of increasing tea yield rate in India during the period. This evident from the Table No. 5 of the study.

Table 5. Average Yield Rate in India (1996)

State	*1984*	*1985*	*1986*	*1993*	*1994*	*1995*	*1996*
Assam	1576	1639	1507	1770	1764	1751	1824
West Bengal	1516	1606	1426	1619	1589	1593	1621
Total North India	1514	1446	1540	1697	1679	1671	1731
Total South India	2009	1926	1868	2372	2107	2117	2050
Total India	1606	1645	1523	1819	1768	1763	1796

Source : Ibid., 9-10.

It is observed from the Table No. 5 of the study that there was every possibility of increasing yield rate in all over the country. To supplement this, let us see the Table No. 6 of the study.

Table 6. Potentiality of Production Increase (1996)

Sl.No.	*Region*	*Area in Hect.*	*Highest Yield (in Kg/Hec.)*	*Average Yield (in Kg/Hec.)*	*Additional Production (in Mil. Kg.)*
1.	Assam	231942	—	1770	269.80
2.	West Bengal	100489	—	1619	100.94
3.	North India	342789	—	1696	375.51
4.	South India	75542	3833	2373	110.29
	All India	418331	—	1819	485.50

Source: CCPA : 1996 : 8.

It is evident from the Table No. 6 of the study that another 485.50 million kilograms of tea could be produced in India till 2000 A.D. if proper land utilisation could have been done.

Table 7. Land Availability and Utilization (1995-1996)

Sl. No.	*Region*	*No. of Garden*	*Within Grant Land*			*Outside Grant Land*	
			Area under Tea	*Fallow Land*	*Available for extension*	*Vested*	*Degraded*
1.	Assam	304	137808	3778	10491	10507	2537
2.	West Bengal	157	64059	2744	5052	4806	2277
3.	Total North India	463	202554	6536	15714	15420	4813
4.	Total All India	549	241631	7031	16811	16972	16050

Source : Ibid.

Interestingly, the Table No. 7 of the study portrays the fact that 549 gardens had 7031 hectares of fallow land and 16811 hectares of land available for extension within their grant land. Similarly, it is also observed that there is 16,972 hectares of land as government vest land and 16,050 hectares of land as degraded forest land outside the grant areas of these 549 tea gardens.

Tea Consumption

Tea is the most important beverage around the world. Let us see the nature of consumption pattern of Indian tea in domestic as well as foreign markets. It was found that in 1996 India produced 780 million kilograms of which 613 million kilograms was sold in the domestic market and only 106 million kilograms of tea had been exported whereas Srilanka exported around 220 million kilograms in the foreign markets. If the same trend could continue then it was expected that by 1998 it would come down further to 158 million kilograms of tea. On the basis of that some future protections were made for the Indian tea industry by CCPA, Calcutta in 1996.

Table 8. Projection on Future Consumption

Year	*Production*	*Domestic Consumption (in Million Kg.)*	*Exportable Surplus (in Million Kg.)*
1996	780	613	166
1997	781	632	159
1998	809	651	158
1999	838	671	167
2000	874	692	182
2001	912	713	199
2002	950	734	216
2003	990	756	234
2004	1021	778	234
2005	1071	801	270
2006	1111	824	270

Source : Ibid., 6.

Quite interestingly, it is observed from the Table No. 8

of the study that till 1998, the production would be gone down due to lack of replanting and rejuvenation as well as uprooting activities. But from 1999 onward it was expected that there would be a wide coverage of tea export to 167 million kilograms by 2006. Similarly, in production scenario also, there would be around 1111 million kilograms by 2006 in India.

Some Projections

To improve the production scenario, the following considerations were given top priority (CCPA: 1996: 4) :

1. Its operations were basically agriculture in nature depending upon the weather conditions for sustained increase in production.
2. Its long gestation period—a newly planted tea bush took five to eight years to achieve full potency or maturity.
3. Periodic decline in crop levels to sustain long term investment proposals.
4. Remunerative price levels to sustain long term investment proposals.
5. The availability of land for extension planting.
6. The loss in crop and therefore income arising from replanting and rejuvenation prunning.
7. The characteristics of each tea growing district are different and generalisations may led to misleading results.
8. Five years target setting for the tea industry could not be made without leading to distorted results-any projection or target fixing should be made over a minimum span of ten years and preferably over fifteen years.

One of the important issues before making any expansion projection of tea industry is to identify the suitable land available around the plantations which is very tough business. The Consultative Committee of Plantation Associations, Calcutta reports that interms of present total area under tea, the coverage was about 57.0%. In North India, the availability was 22,250 hectares in respect of 463 estates while 86 tea estates in South India reported available of 1,592 hectares. Interestingly, inspite of having such land, the tea gardens have not been able to utilise these land for tea cultivation. It is also observed that almost 10.0% of land were distributed to the manpower resources of the plantations which remain barren almost throughout the year.

Another important problem to make an accurate projection was due to non-availability of exact figures because many of these tea estates do not have regular land title deeds or have not been able to register themselves either with the state government or the Tea Board of India due to restriction under the land ceiling acts. However, an analysis has been made on the tea which is basically revenue paying product of the country. This will be evident from the Table No. 9 of the study.

Table 9. Future Projection on Production, Domestic Consumption and Exportable Surplus (Million kg.)

Year	*Production*	*Domestic Consumption*	*Exportable Surplus*
1996	780	613	172
1997	804	632	172
1998	821	651	170
1999	840	671	169
2000	858	692	166
2001	876	713	163
2002	895	734	161
2003	915	756	159
2004	934	778	156
2005	954	801	153
2006	974	824	151

Source : Ibid., 6.

It is transparent from the Table No. 9 of the study that the exportable surplus is likely to decline over the next decades. If we wanted to maintain export to the tune of 200 million kilograms by 2000 A.D., then another 30 to 35 million kilograms of tea was to be added. It was therefore projected that during next ten to fifteen years, there would be no pressure on supplies to meet the domestic consumption. Since India had accepted for globalization of Indian economy, the exports were to be encouraged. In this context, tea industry might contribute a lot if exports were to be increased considerably.

2

Small Growers and New Plantations in Nineties

As discussed in the chapter I that tea export was to be improved during the nineties of 19th century. One of the encouraging developments taking place then was the role of small growers ever since 1989 in India. The Tea Board of India defined "Small Grower" as the plantation having 8.09 hectares (20 acres) of land. However, for all practical purposes, the nomenclature covered the gardens upto 50 hectares without having manufacturing or processing unit. According to Tea Board of India (1996), there were 10,748 small growers in South India having 8.09 hectares of land (CCPA: 1996 : 8). Interestingly, it was found that there were over 300 small growers in North Bengal and between 7,000 to 20,000 small growers in Assam. Incidently, the number of such small growers were not incorporated in any record-both government and other organisations.

The Small growers had their unique problems of their own. So, let us discuss their problems which are still there and then assess their contributions towards the national economy. However, these problems are different in different regions of the country.

Emergence of Small Growers in North Bengal of North-East India

In 1973-74, certain enterprising persons in North Bengal discovered a large tract of fallow land in Siliguri sub-division of Darjeeling district, Jalpaiguri and North Dinajpur, the then West Dinajpur, under the ownership of village dwellers. After the thorough persuasion with the local people, those lands were brought under the cultivation by providing employment to local unemployed youths. The tea gardens grown in those tracts earned handsome profits which also attracted the native village pineapple growers who also started establishing small grower gardens. However, such success became short-lived due to over production without adequate preservation or marketing facilities. That caused a good many small tea growers to revert to their original pineapple cultivation. With the price boon on tea in 1989-90, the Tea Board of India felt it indespensible to cultivate tea in fallow land. The process had now gathered sufficient momentum.

Location of Small Grower Gardens

The small grower gardens were mainly located at the Islampur sub-division of North Dinajpur district of West Bengal. There was a small garden called Debijhora till 1988-89 but after 1998, this garden had converted into small grower garden as they had Kusum, Sarot and Ramboti small grower gardens in the area. Observing the success of those gardens, small growers had been established in Sonapur locality which extend upto Daspara in an almost continuous stretch along the Indo-Bangladesh border. Here, in this context, a few well established tea company such as Terai Land Project of Duncans, Longview Tea and Gangabari Tea estates. The Jayshree and Bijoynagar Tea companies had also started making small grower gardens. After that, the size of small grower gardens had been classified into two categories, viz,—first, the gardens having land between 15 to 100 acres under big tea companies as mentioned above and secondly, those gardens which had 2 to 15 acres under the local people of the villages. The basic difference between the two types of gardens was that former type of owners had exclusive profit margin while the later group took tea cultivation because of assurance of better income over what they used to get from pineapple agriculture in their marginal land holdings (*Ibid* : 9).

Pioneering such small grower gardens, certain problems had been evolved during the early phase of globalization due to the purchase of lands by middlemen of big companies. In some cases, drains had been dug which took the water away from the prime agricultural land and then the local people were forced to sell their land. That caused agrarian movement in the region which enforced the government to come up with the land policy in early 1990 which formulated the following conditions to establish such small grower gardens in the region.

1. It was not to be prime agricultural land.
2. It was not to be tribal land.
3. It did not fall within the Teesta Command Area.
4. It was not to be the forest land.

With the government notification, the local people, trade unions and local panchayats assessed the socio-economic conditions or implications of those small grower gardens and finally a consensus came out accordingly. Under the consensus, the land in which the plantations were established lie along the border areas in mixed high and low areas. The local people called those lands as "Malbhumi Jami" as nothing could be grown in those areas. One of those areas was even called Barran lands which to the people had low social value as those lands were the gate of smuggling across the Indo-Bangladesh border. Those people got employment in those tea gardens throughout the year. Similarly, it was also realised that there was enough scope to expand the plantations to South of Islampur area of North Bengal. In this direction, adequate scope was also given to the small growers to sell their green tea leaves. In certain pockets of Jalpaiguri district, the small growers were increasing by leaps and bounds.

Numerical Strength of Small Growers

As mentioned above, there were over 300 small grower tea estates in North Bengal. This is evident from the following Table No. 10. In this table, we have seen the gardens of 2 to 100 acres size only.

Table 10. Number of Small Grower Garden (1996)

S.No.	*District*	*No. of Garden*	*Total Area (in Hectare)*	*Planted Area*	*Green Leaf Crop (in lakh Kg.)*
1.	Jalpaiguri	21	340	168	21
2.	Darjeeling (Siliguri)	26	308	152	19
3.	Uttar Dinaspur	80	920	480	60
	Total	127	1608	800	100

Source : Ibid., 10.

Apart from the 127 tea estates, 8 more gardens were expected to come up very shortly during 1997. Altogether, those would be of 400 hectares of land with 20 lakhs kilograms of tea leaves. If it was so, then total area would come to 2000 hectares with 120 lakhs green tea leaf. It was also observed that if the trend would continue then there would have been 3500 hectares of land with 134.55 lakh kilograms of green leaf.

In Dooars also, there were 1350 hectares of land under the small grower gardens with at least 25 lakh green leaf. On the basis of above discussion, it was projected that there would be almost 30 million kilograms of made tea with growth rate of 3500 kilograms per hectare from new plantations if these new plantations would be continued with the same tampo at least till 2000 A.D.

Selling of Green Leaf

Unlike larger estates which had their respective factories to manufacture their green leaf, the small growers had to sell their leaf to the neighbouring established gardens. However, during 1997, two bought leaf factories had been established at Bidhannager and Kartowa. Still two more factories had come up in the same year. Some of the tea estates such as Jayantika, Sayedabad, Kamalpur, Kiran Chandra and Taipo also purchased green leaf from small growers. In that context, the local trade unions were suggesting the owners of small grower gardens to open up a cooperative factory for those small grower gardens. Again, there appeared to have been some problems in selling the green leaf for the small growers as they got Rs. 7 only per kilogram of green leaf. In fact, green leaf price used to depend on the auction price rates of the market.

Problems of Small Growers

Similar to the established tea gardens, the small growers had problems relating to acquiring "No Objection Certificate" from the Government of West Bengal. Till 1999, only 19 estates could obtain the certificate. Again, those small growers who had factories had not been able to obtain the certificate. Legally, if any estate had not obtained the certificate, then it could not be registered to Tea Board of India and it could not approach any bank or financial institutions for loans. Therefore, whatever capital to be invested was to be generated from within the small growers only. In such circumstances, the growth of the industry could not be guaranteed. Another important reason for not being registered was that those areas came under the Teesta Command Area though not officially defined.

Another important problem of those small growers was water management in Terai and Uttar Dinajpur areas. Yet some areas were water-logged and proper drainage system was to be done. That had caused Rs. 6,500 cost per hectare for drainage and a sum of Rs. 97,000 for irrigation resulting which a total of Rs. 80 lakhs had to spend for irrigation and drainage system.

Still another problem faced by the small growers was that they could not extend plantations due to the restriction imposed by the Border Security Force in the international border. Because of that, about 35 square kilometers of land were remaining unutilised. Those growers were lacking to get technical expertise either from Tea Research Associations or any other technical institutions because of high subscription charged by them. So, the small growers had listed their needs as follows :

1. To provide financial assistance for the small growers on easy terms and conditions and at low rate of interest.
2. To remove non-technical constraints, *i.e.*, granting No Objection Certificate, land conversion to the small growers.
3. To arrange for training of manpower with respect of the following aspects.

(*a*) Pest Management, (*b*) Weed Management, (*c*) Soil and Water Management, (*d*) Plucking, (*e*) Prunning, (*f*) Cultivation Practices, (*g*) Cost Effectiveness in Cultural Operation, (*h*) Soil Testing, (*i*) Routine Technology, (*j*) Setting up of Manufacturing factory.

Keeping above needs in toto, the viable option that had left to the small growers was to get assistance from technical institutes and motivational trainings from different organisations. By doing so, the cost effectiveness of the production could be minimised.

Small Growers in Assam Valley

The history of small growers in Assam was more or less same as of North Bengal. There, this crop attracted the attention of educated unemployed youths and even service holders. The small growers had been expanded in Goalpara, Kokrajhar, Dhubri, Karbi Anglong etc. in Assam, Altogether, as per All Assam Small Tea Growers Association, there were 4028 tea growers of small category with 15.7 thousand hectares of land. That sector provided self employment to 8500 people of the state of Assam. Let us see the district-wise small tea growers till December, 1996.

Table 11. Small Growers in Assam (in Hectare)

Sl. No.	*District*	*Number of Garden*	*Percentage*
1.	Tinsukia	227	9.2%
2.	Dibrugargh	852	34.5%
3.	Sibsagar	439	17.3%
4.	Jorhat	321	13.1%
5.	Golaghat	446	18.1%
6.	Naongaon	12	0.5%
7.	Morigaon	11	0.4%
8.	Sonitpur	24	1.0%
9.	Lakhimpur	17	0.7%
10.	Dhemaji	01	0.1%
11.	Kamrup	18	0.7%
12.	Goalpara	72	3.0%
13.	Kokrajhar	01	0.1%
14.	Karbi Anglong	22	0.1%
15.	Dhubri	02	0.1%
16.	Danay	01	0.1%

Source : Ibid., 16.

It is observed from the Table No. 11 of the study that number of small grower tea gardens had concentrated in Dibrugargh, Sibsagar, Jorhat and Golaghat. Those gardens had got constant assistance from Assam Agricultural University. Hardly, any study had so far been made on those small growers excepting two post-graduate research studies conducted by the Assam Agricultural University. Studies as mentioned had found that the land owned by the small growers was mainly their own land, government vested land, grazing land and ceiling surplus land. Previously, the owned land was under sugarcane, bamboo gardens, coconut, nut (Tambul) and other types of trees. It was also found from the studies that average tea holding areas varied from 0.632 hectares to 9.53 hectares. Interestingly, it was also observed that 43.0% to 53.0% of total population of the areas got jobs in the plantations. Each garden was earning Rs. 40,000 per year per hectare after deducting the cost effectiveness (expenditure) of Rs. 72,000 per hectare per year.

Problems of Assam Small Tea Growers

Following were the main problems of Assam Small Tea Growers during early nineties:

1. Encroachment of Government vested land, Government grazing land etc.
2. Lack of government certificate for tea cultivation.
3. Lack of financial assistance from various sources.
4. Sale of green leaf with required prices.
5. Production cost of green leaf was much above the manufacturing tea.
6. Lack of cooperative factory.
7. Lack of interest of big estates to purchase green leaf.
8. Theft of green leaf.

Considering the above apparent problems of the small growers in Assam, certain suggestions were put forwarded by the Calcutta Consultative Committee of Plantation Associations in 1996. They were as follows :

A. Cooperative Tea Processing units or factories might be established.

B. Technical know - how training would be given to the small growers.

C. Credit from Tea Board of India and other financial institutions would be given.

D. Assistance from the World Bank would be given.

E. Rationalisation and Modernisation programmes would be done.

F. Establishment of Small Grower Mutual Assistance Groups and Associations would be formed.

Small Growers in South India

Tea industry was started in South India in the last century but the history of small growers was the new phenomenon of early eighties of 19th century. Such small growers were found in Nilgiri, Induki, Wynad and limited area in Chimanglur districts.

Table 12. Structure of Small Growers in South India (1996)

Sl.No.	*Land Holding No.*	*Units*	*Area in Hectare*
1.	More than 400 hectares	36	18,659
2.	200-400 hectares	107	31,109
3.	100-200 hectares	54	8.123
4.	50 to 100 hectares	51	2.297
5.	10 to 50 hectares	205	3,547
6.	Less than 10 hectares	47,500	22,809
	Total	47,943	86,544

Source : Ibid., 20.

The Table 12 of the study indicates that the gardens of 200 to 400 hectares size were highest in South India. Altogether, there were 22,809 hectares under tea having 1,756 kilograms of made tea per hectare while large growers had the capacity to produce 2,290 kilograms per hectare in South India. The low productivity rate of small growers was due to the absence of adequate awareness on scientific cultivation, method and other financial constraints.

The Then Projections Made on Small Growers for South India

1. Diversification of area considering weather conditions.
2. Replanting of bushes as there were 2375 hectares of land available for replanting in small sectors.
3. Increase in bush population.

4. There was the scope of another 500 hectares for new plantations, 5350 hectares for infilling, 4080 hectares for rejuvenation and 2375 hectares for replanting in South India.
5. Constant assistance was to be taken from Tea Board of India for finance and other assistance.

If those works were done then there was every scope for small growers to increases another 61 million kilograms of tea by 2000 A.D. However, later on the number of small grower gardens increased by leaps and bound but the problems cited above are still found in adequate manner. The other facets of small growers have been discussed in later chapters of the study.

3

Early Phase of Globalization and Plantation Workers

The tea plantation workers were mainly the immigrants or the descendents of immigrants from various parts of the country and even neighbouring countries. The indegeneous people of Assam, Bengal and South India did not accept the works in the plantations due to low wages and isolation from the mainstream (Bhowmik : 1981). The history of their immigration is normally dates back to early 18th century. The tea garden workers in Assam and Dooars were mainly the tribals from Bihar, Orissa and Madhya Pradesh (Kar : 1981) while the entire work force of Darjeeling hills were exclusively the local Nepalis (Sharma : 1997).

Discussing the features of the plantation workers, Bhowmik (1981) has stated that low wage, coercion and isolation were common among all the workers besides the indenture nature of recruitment. This might be the apparent reason why still the tea gardens are isolated enclaves and they have got their own type of plantation system of democracy. In the initial period of the plantations, they were recruited by the plantation Sardars who used to recruit respective caste and tribal members from their native villages (Sharma : 1997). To attract them in the plantations, the females and child workers were also recruited so that they could not run away from the occupational hazards of the plantation system. To maintain their closeness, even some paramilitary forces were administered around the plantations by the colonial planters. The armed forces were disbanded on 14th August, 1947 (Bhowmik: 1981). Another reason for having the tea garden enclaves which were successfully sustained for ever was due to the heterogeneous nature of castes or tribal agrarian background of the workers. Each caste or tribe had their distinct dialect which could not be understood by another castes or tribes of the plantations. Thus, to continue the heterogeneous social structure, separate caste or tribal labour lines were made so that two or more castes or tribes could not unite together for common purpose and to struggle against the management for their rights or justice while the management was powerful and united (Sharma : 1997).

The socio-economic conditions of the workers continued unchanged till the eve of independence of the country. After 1947, trade union movement started in tea plantations of Assam, Bengal and South India. That along with the enactment of the Plantation Labour Act, 1951 and other subsequent labour legislations, the tea garden workers also started doing collective bargaining and at even the present time all the agreements are being done by collective bergaining method. But on the other hand, the planters had started declining the number of permanent workers especially after 1951 and during the early nineties of 19th century, more than fifty percent of permanent workers were regular workers while fifty percent workers were temporary and casuals to whom the benefits of various acts were not to be provided (Bhowmik : 1996).

The socio-economic conditions of the plantation workers numbering about eleven lakhs of today can be understood from the nature of the provisions of various labour acts related to the plantation workers during nineties of 19th century. The eleven lakhs tea plantation workers constitute one-seventh of the 70 lakhs total workers of the country of the period. The plantation workers were most exploited sections of workers in the organized sector of the country. The literacy level of the workers was very low.

Though there was no crude form of exploitation of labour during the era due to the emergence of trade union and collective bargaining yet the workers were not known of their rights as enshrined in the various labour legislations applicable to them. As mentioned above, another important dimension of the workers was that those acts were not readable to the grass root level exploited tea plantation workers of the country. Yet another dimension was that half of the plantation workers were females who did not at all got time to realise their justice due to their double role as plantation workers and housewives (Bhadra : 1997). Though the plantation workers were permanent, their wages were calculated as per the Minimum wages Act, 1948 and therefore Minimum Wages Board had been established consisting of the representatives of workers, management and government. In fact, they were daily rated workers of the agro-based industry of the country.

Table 13. Tea Plantation Workers (1996)

Sl. No.	*State*	*Total Workers*
1.	Assam	5,74,088
2.	West Bengal	2,59,783
3.	Total North India (other than Assam and Bengal)	18,363
4.	South India (Kerala, Tamil Nadu and Karnataka)	25,043
	Total	11,02,377

Source : CCPA: 1996.

The Table No. 13 of the study indicates that 77.0% of workers were in the northern states while only 33.0% of them were in the southern states of Tamil Nadu, Kerala and Karnataka.

The Table No. 14 indicates that the number of tea plantation workers had been increased considerably with the increase of number of tea gardens in the country. It was also transparent that during the period from 1961 to 1991, the

Table 14. The Plantation Workers (1951 to 1995)

Year	*Number of Worker*
1951	9,33,497
1961	8,22,834
1971	7,66,593
1981	8,49,206
1991	9,96,735
1992	9,91,704
1993	9,91,019
1994	10,28,699
1995	10,63,801

Source : Tea Digest: 1996 : 1-2.

number of tea plantation workers decreased considerably due to Indo-Chinese, Indo-Pakistan wars and Bangladesh War of liberation.

Tea Plantation Workers in Small Grower Sectors

With the opening of small grower tea gardens, quite a good number of unemployed youths had been employed in those tea plantations. Take for instance of North Bengal where more than 127 tea gardens were there till December, 1996.

Table 15. Workers in Small Grower Sectors (1996)

Sl. No.	*District*	*Number of Workers*	*Percentage*
1.	Jalpaiguri	525	21.0%
2.	Darjeeling (Siliguri)	475	19.0%
3.	Uttar Dinajpur	1500	60.0%

Source : CCPA : 1996.

The Table No. 15 of the study shows that 60.0% of small grower tea garden workers were employed in Uttar Dinajpur gardens while Jalpaiguri had accommodated 21.0% of workers and Siliguri sub-division of Darjeeling district had accommodated 19.0% of the workers. However, it is known from those small growers that till December, 1997, there were more than fifteen thousand workers in North Bengal small grower gardens.

As it was known that besides that small grower tea gardens, new plantations had also established in North Bengal. Consequent upon the introduction of new plantations, the percentage of tea plantation workers had been increased considerably. This is evident from the table No. 16 of the study.

Table 16. Tea Plantation Workers in New Tea Plantations (1996)

Sl. No.	*District*	*No. of Garden*	*Total Area (in Hec.)*	*Planted Area (in Hec.)*	*Workers*	*Percentage*
1.	Jalpaiguri	32	1750	620	1790	13.2%
2.	Darjeeling (Siliguri)	30	400	180	560	4.2%
3.	Uttar Dinajpur	221	6330	3846	11.220	82.6%
	Total	283	8480	4650	13.570	100.0%

Source : Ibid., 12.

The Table No. 16 of the study indicates that Uttar Dinajpur district had accommodated 92.6% of the workers in new tea plantations while the Jalpaiguri district and Siliguri of Darjeeling district had accommodated 13.2% and 4.2% respectively. According to a study of All Assam Tea Growers Association, there were 10,160 workers employed in those new tea plantations. Interestingly, it is also observed that all the workers in those new plantations unlike in the old plantations were the native people who were completely engaged in agrarian activities of the regions.

Wages of the Workers

The wages of the tea plantation workers were like today

was determined on the resolutions of the tripartite agreements for tea workers at the interval of every three years. The nature of agreement used to vary from one state to another depending upon the legal situations. Being daily rated workers, their wages were calculated for six days a week.

Table 17. Daily Wages of the Workers

State	*Daily Adult*	*Wage (in Rs.) Child*	*Incentive (Paise)*	*Quata (in Kg.)*
Assam (Average of all zones)	25.60	13.80	34	21
West Bengal	26.30	13.00	32	21–31
Tamil Nadu	42.00	25.00	26–42	14–20
Kerala	44.00	27.00	30–35	18–20

Source : Bhowmik : 1996.

The plantation workers were paid wages for time as well as piece work. The table No. 17 of the study shows that the wage rate varied from one state to another. Similarly, incentive rate for extra leaf plucked also varied from one state to another. Recently in 1996, in West Bengal, the wages of the plantation workers had been increased by a tripartite agreement. According to that agreement, then from April 1997 to March, 1998, each worker would get the wage of Rs. 29.30. In the second year, the wage would reached to Rs. 32.30 and in the third year, it would be Rs. 34.80. The agreement of 1997 had been implemented from April, 1997 and it would be applied till March, 2000 A.D. The workers were assured to pay their arrears by December, 1997. But interestingly, the enhanced wages was much lower than Tamil Nadu and Kerala, Moreover, the incentives of the workers were limited for three to four months of the year when plucking of tea leaves were done at the maximum level. Besides wages, the tea plantation workers had been provided other facilities through different labour acts.

Among other acts applicable to the plantation workers, the Plantation Labour Act, 1951 was most important piece of labour legislation for tea plantation workers of the country. Let us see the various provisions of the Plantation Labour Act, 1951 along with other related labour acts applicable to tea plantation workers of the country.

The Plantation Labour Act, 1951

To protect the plantation workers of the country, for the first time, the Government of India enacted this act. The act is considered to be the landmark of the development of the plantation workers in the country. The act provided specific provisions for regulating the working and living conditions of the workers. It also restricts the employers from inhuman behaviour to the employees of the plantations.

The Indian Parliament enacted the act in October, 1951 but it came into force from 1954 only. The act was widely accepted by workers and trade unions but management were not happy with the act as they said that the act involves additional substantial amount of money to be paid to the workers. But after a few years, the Menon Commission on Tea industry (1957) found that the financial burden on employers was very low of 12 paise per kilogram of made tea. However, due to the then price crisis of tea, government considered the problem of the employers. That was the main reason why the act could be implemented from 1954 only. Unfortunately, inspite of having this act, there was hardly any tea garden where the entire provisions of this act had been fully implemented till the implementation of Liberalisation, Privatisation and Globalization policy of government in 1991. However, this act is still on vogue. Let us discuss the main provisions of the act to inform the workers that formally they are still protected. Before discussing the provisions, we should keep in mind that the act had been amended twice in 1971 and 1982. Yet another bill was lying in the floor of Parliament ever since 1991. Sections are mentioned as Sec. and clauses as CL. To give more realistic application of the act, state government had made respective plantation labour rules. In West Bengal, we have West Bengal Plantation Labour Rules, 1956. Similarly, Assam and Tripura have their respective plantation labour rules, 1956.

The act defines a 'Plantation' as a piece of land of five hectares (fifteen acres) or more in size which is being used to cultivate tea, coffee, rubber, cinchona or cardamom and on which fifteen or more persons have been employed for even a single day during the last twelve months (Sec. 1, Cl. 4 (*a*) and (*b*). The act has also defined plantation worker as the person who has been employed by the management to do any work which is skilled, unskilled, manual or clerical. The person must not have drawn above Rs. 750 per month during the first decade of globalization. The people in the managerial categories and medical officials were not considered as workers even if they were drawing less than Rs. 750 per month. Besides that, any person who had been engaged in construction of buildings, roads, bridges etc. within the plantations could not be called a plantation worker (Sec. 2, Cl. k). The plantation labour Act, 1951 has classified the plantation workers into three categories:

1. Adult : Any Male or Female worker who has completed 18 years of age (Sec. 2, b).
2. Adolescent: A worker who is either male or female who has completed 14 years of age (Sec. 2, a).
3. Child : A worker who is either male or female and who is less than 14 years of age (Sec. 2, a).

Interestingly, it is found that in West Bengal, child worker was paid just the half wage to that of the adult worker while in South India each child worker was paid two third of the wage that of the adult worker.

One of the important provisions of PLA was related to regulating the work hour of the workers. According to this provision, an adult worker has to work for 48 hours in a week for his or her minimum wages. It means a worker must not work more than 8 hours a day and six days in a week. The child and adolescent workers must not work more than 27 hours per week and four hours and thirty minutes every day for six days. The act has also stated that no adult worker should work more than five hours at a stretch. Workers must be provided at least half an hour rest every day (Sec. 21).

The act permits adult worker of male category to work either at day or night but women and child workers can not be asked by the employers to work during the night time, *i.e.*, between 6 P.M. to 7 A.M. (Sec. 25). It is obligatory on the part of management to notify the period of work so that the workers can know the timing and place of work, well in advance (Sec. 23, 1). The Rule 74 of West Bengal Plantation Labour Rules also states that the notice has to be given through Form No. 6 in which time, place and hour of work of workers are written by the management. The notice has to be displayed at an appropriate place so that the workers can read it in time. The notice has to be written at least in two languages, *i.e.*, English and the language easily understood by the majority of the workers.

Considering weather conditions of the plantations, the act has stated that employers have to provide protective clothing against rain and cold. For instance, in West Bengal, blankets, pullovers, umbrellas, shoes etc. are to be given to the workers at free of cost (WBPLR: 72).

No employer can ask his or her workers to work more than 6 days a week as one day is rest day to be given to the workers. The Rule No. 73 of WBPLR has stated that Sunday should be holiday for the workers. The employer may however substitute another day of the week for holiday. Supposing any worker works on the rest day, he or she will be paid over time at his or her rate of twice the daily wages.

Every plantation worker is entitled to earned leave. An adult worker will get one earned leave for every 20 days of his or her work. Here, the adolescent and child workers are entitled to one day earned leave for every 15 days work. In this context, even half day work is considered one earned leave for the day of the year. The earned leave is not counted on regular holidays (Sec. 30). Provided a worker does not utilise his or her leave fully during the year, the excess leave will be carried over to next year or another three years. However, the total number of days is restricted to 30 days (Sec. 30(2) and (3). The earned leave is the holiday with full wages which is to be paid by the management before the workers left for holiday (31 Sec. (*a*). During the leave period, workers are to be given other facilities such as ration, fuel etc. The same is also to be given to the monthly rated workers (Sec. 31, *a*). The leave wages will be the average wages of the workers during the calender year. But the overtime wages are excluded. Similarly, Bonus are excluded here in the leave wages. The worker will be entitled to cash value of his or her earned leave if he or she is going to retire or terminated from the services.

Every worker who has put in six or more months of service is entitled to rent free housing facilities within the plantation. To get the free house, a worker has to inform the management in written form and the management has to provide a separate house for each worker and his family (Sec. 15). The Housing Advisory Committee of state government sets forth the standards and specifications of the houses. The committee consists of four representatives each of management, trade unions and government (Rule: WBPLR: 57). At present, the specification of workers' houses are: two rooms, one of 10 feet × 12 feet and another of 8 feet × 10 feet, one kitchen of 4 × 6 feet, one Varandah of 4 feet × 6 feet. The houses must have their separate latrines. The houses are to be made of walls of cement and bricks with roof of corrugated iron sheets or asbestos. No rent has to be charged for the houses (Rule WBPLR: 53). Further, Plantation Labour Act makes it very clear that it is compulsory for the management of the plantations to maintain the houses (Sec. 16 A). The repair works are to be done at least once in a year. Here if the worker dies or injures due to poor maintenance of house than the person's kin can claim compensation under the Workman's Compensation Act or at the recommendation of the Labour Commissioner on receipt of the application within six months from the kins of the injured or dead person (Sec. 16 C).

The Plantation Labour Act, 1951 states that health facilities to the workers not only mean the medical facilities but also drinking water and sanitation. The employer is bound to provide sufficient drinking water at the places nearer to the houses of the workers (Sec. 8). The WBPLR state that the drinking water is to be supplied from reliable source as approved by the plantation inspector (Rule 10). If the drinking water is supplied from the well then it should be free of pollution (Rule 12). It means that water tanks must be properly covered and this is to be made for drinking and not for washing clothes and bathing. The Paniwalas should supply drinking water to the workers at their places of work. The PLA has also stated that the labour lines must be provided drinking water, separate latrines and urinals for males and females must be properly cleaned and maintained (Sec. 9(1) and (2). For instance, WBPLR has specified that every plantation must have latrine for every 50 acres of cultivated land and half of these latrines is to be given to the females (Rule 15). The latrines are to be daily cleaned and such latrines are to be made on the approval of Public Health Authority. The employer must also made Puccka drains so as to clear waste and dirty water.

As per the act, all the workers are entitled to free medical facilities for themselves and their families. The family includes the worker and his or her spouse, dependent children (those who are below 18 years of age) and dependent parents (Sec. 10). The medical facility is to be given at free of cost. Besides, the workers are also entitled to medical allowance in case they are sick and cannot report to duty. There are two types of hospitals in West Bengal in tea growing areas. Firstly, there are garden hospitals which will deal with the cases not requiring major medical treatment and care. Secondly, there are Group Hospitals that deal with mostly serious cases. In any plantation where there are more than 1000 workers, a hospital should be there with 15 beds. Again, the plantation having less than 1000 workers may share the hospital of neighbouring garden. In such case, there should be dispensary. Again, the plantations with less than 200 workers must have first aid box with medicines as specified by the plantation inspector. The WBPLR has specified that there should be a qualified doctor, a trained Dhai, a mid-wife, a qualified compounder and a trained health assistant.

Their services are to be given at all time of the day and night. The plantations which have only dispensaries must have a trained compounder, nurse and medical assistant. The gardens located in the interior places having 350 workers must have dispensaries with 5 detention beds under the charge of full time compounder. The medicines and other equipments at the dispensaries are to be procured as per the specification of Medical Advisory Board set up by the state government. The Board will have the representation of trade unions, management and government. It reviews the progress of health facilities and make necessary recommendations to the employers.

Every worker is entitled to sickness allowance provided he or she produces sickness certificate from the medical practioner of the plantation (Sec. 31). Women workers are entitled to Maternity benefits allowances. For instance, in West Bengal, every worker can get sickness allowance for a period of 15 days in every year. This allowance will be at the rate of two-third of the worker's wage but not be less than Re. 1 per day for adults and 75 paise for others. In case a worker does not take sickness allowance for one year then it will be carried over to next three years. The total number of sickness leave does not exceed 30 days.

The plantation having 50 women workers or 20 children below the age of six years, there should be creche for the children under the charge of a qualified Dhai or attendant. The creches must be clean, airy and has to function while the mothers are at work. There is to be a wash room for the children in the creches. The WBPLR states that the employers have to provide 75 ml. Clean milk and refreshments (biscuits and bread) to each child daily. Clean clothes are to be provided to the creche staff.

To educate the children below 12 years and above 6 years, the employers have to provide free primary schools within the plantation areas, with qualified teachers. However, primary school can be set up only when there are more than 25 or more children in the age group of 6 to 12 years within the plantation (Sec. 14).

The plantation employing 150 workers or more must have one or more canteens where the workers can buy tea and snacks at the reasonable rate (Sec. 11). The canteen is to run on no-profit-no-loss basis and prices of items are to be displayed in screen every day. There should be canteen committee which will supervise the canteen for its proper functioning. The committee will have representatives of the workers also.

The act directs the employer to provide recreational facilities to the workers (Sec. 13). The recreational facilities include indoor and outdoor games suitable to adults and children. The playground should be there in the plantation.

However, the above discussion made it clear that the act does not provide any protection for workers who are handling dangerous chemicals such as pesticides, weedicides etc. So, what is needed today is to provide proper protective medical facilities to the workers who handle these chemicals and pesticides in the plantations. This requires proper trainings to the workers by the management and employers of the plantations.

Besides the Plantation Labour Act, 1951, there are other acts such as Maternity Act, 1961, Minimum Wages Act, 1948, Industrial Disputes Act, 1947, Payment of Gratuity Act, 1965, Payment of Bonus Act, 1972, Employees Provident Fund Act, 1952 etc. which are also applicable to the plantation industry. In this section, we will discuss some of the acts which are directly related to the plantation industry and its workers in order to understand as to how far these workers come under the purview of the industrial sector of the country.

Maternity Benefit Act

Almost fifty percent of plantation workers are females. This act is therefore very important for women workers who are engaged in tea plantation. It grants protection to women workers especially at the time of pregnancy and child delivery. Normally, women workers are cheated and not given facilities which has affected their health and thereafter their works at the gardens and homes are adversely affected.

According to the act, a woman worker when she is pregnant is entitled to have leave with fully pay for certain period before and after her delivery. It is the duty of employer to pay her full wages (Sec. 5(1) in addition to some other cash benefits.

As per the act, a pregnant woman worker is entitled for 6 weeks before and 6 weeks after the delivery leaves 5(3). It means that altogether 12 weeks of leave with fully pay is to be given to the women workers. The payment of her wages are calculated on the average of wages payable for the days she worked during the three months proceeding to date from which she takes leave. The over-time wages are not included here in this case (Sec. 5(1). It is to be clearly noted that average wage includes both time (Hazira) as well as piece (Doubli). The worker is entitled to free medical care before and after delivery. If such care is not given then a sum of Rs. 250 is to be given to the worker (Sec. 8).

However, to avail the benefits, every woman worker has to work for 80 days in a year preceeding the date of her delivery (Sec. 5(2)). In order to get this facility, the worker has to give notice to the employer regarding the expected date of the delivery with the name of her nominee to receive dues if she is not able to receive it (Sec. 6(2). If she has not given this notice earlier, then the same is to be given to the employer after her delivery (Sec. 6(8). On receipt of her notice, employer is bound to pay her dues within 48 hours (Sec. 6(5).

If unfortunately, a woman worker undergoes miscarriage, she will be entitled to the leave on production of proof of miscarriage (Sec. 9). In case of death of a woman worker at the time of delivery, her nominee will be entitled to the amount (Sec. 5(3) and Sec. 7.

Besides the leave as mentioned above, a woman worker is also entitled other facilities. The woman cannot be engaged in any heavy work for one month prior to the six weeks proceeding the delivery (Sec. 4(3).

After resuming her duty, she is entitled to two breaks daily for nursing her child for fifteen months (Sec. 11) in addition to the regular half an hour rest interval. The act also states that a woman worker if she remains absent, her employer cannot dismiss her from her service if she is pregnant (Sec. 12). But she should give notice to her employer.

Finally, the act has also very categorically emphasised that if any employer fails to pay her dues than she must appeal to Assistant Labour Commissioner for redressal. If her claim is found legal and if employer disapproves for payment then ALC can ask district collector to recover the amount from employer from the land revenue of the plantation.

Minimum Wages Act, 1948

As we have already discussed that the plantation workers are mainly paid three types of wages. Firstly, the worker is paid a time-rated wages (Hazira or daily wages) and secondly, a piece rated wage (doubly or extra leaf price). Thirdly, the workers are also paid monthly rate wages. The workers are also given foodgrains at subsidised rates. All these three constitute the minimum wages of the workers (Sec. 4).

The section 15 of the act states that the wages cannot be deducted by the employer if the workers do not do eight hours work in any day of the week. If any employer wants to deduct the wages he has to prove that the worker could not complete his task (work) because he was unwilling to do so. This has to be done on the basis of method specified in the Industrial Disputes Act, 1947. This means that the employer cannot make any prorata deduction on wages if the workers is unable to complete his minimum quota fixed for him on the day.

It is observed that the plantation workers are low paid workers then other types of workers in the country. The main reason lies in computing the minimum wages for the plantation workers. The minimum wages are calculated on the basis of minimum requirement of the workers and two membes of the family. So, what is needed is that while computing minimum wages, the Advisory Board should take into account of minimum needs such as food, clothings and shelter of the workers. Unfortunately for the plantation workers, minimum wages are calculated on the basis of one half units of consumption on the belief that each family has more than one working member in the plantation. This logic does not have any rational implication. This has caused the low wages structure of the plantation workers in India.

Industrial Disputes Act, 1947

Plantation is considered as an industry though basically it is based on agriculture. So, like other industries of the country, plantation workers are also protected by certain laws. The Industrial Disputes Act, 1947 is such an act which provides elaborate official machinery to resolve the disputes between the workers and management. An industrial dispute is meant a dispute or controversy between the workers and employer in regard to the terms and conditions of works. Secondly, the dispute may be related to dismissal, retrenchment or refusal of employment of an individual or individuals by the employer. Again, disputes may be related to legality of any order passed by an employer, application and interpretation of Standing Orders, withdrawal of a benefit, hours of work, and rest interval, issues related to holidays, hours of work and rest interval, issues related to holidays and paid leave, Bonus, (profit sharing), Provident Fund, Gratuity, Classification of grades, Rules of disciplines, changes of work organisation under rationalisation, retrenchment of workers, closure etc. of the establishment. The act prescribed that if an employer proposes to change anything in the industry, he has to give notice to the workmen likely to be effected by the same, he is to forbidden such changes before 42 days in West Bengal and 21 days in other states.

The dispute can be raised by unions and individual worker also. The law provides the following procedure for settlement of individual and collective disputes:

Grievance Settlement Authority

The act provides that every employer who employs fifty or more workers in his/her industry must provide settlement authority for settlement of disputes related to individual workers employed in the industry.

Conciliation

Every individual region has a conciliating officer who is appointed by the state government. A dispute may be referred to him by either of affected parties or he himself if he apprehends a dispute may initiate for conciliatory proceedings. His job is to persuade the disputing parties to arrive at a settlement. He however, has no power to come to directly them nor can he passes an order. If his efforts do not succeed he submits a Failure Report to the government.

Adjudication

The procedure involves labour courts. The government after receiving the Failure Report of the conciliation officer decides whether the case can be referred to a labour court or not refer and settle at its own level. Once it is referred then the court goes through the legal proceedings and gives an award and the award is binding on both the parties. However, if either of the parties is found disatisfied with the award then it can go to High Court or Supreme Court.

Arbitration

The procedure involves independent third party intervention in the case. The employer and aggrieved workers may mutually select an independent person whom they trust, to mediate and resolve the dispute and the decision of the person is final for both the parties. In these days in so far as the plantations are concerned, the conciliation is going to be the best method.

Conciliation Officer

On receipt of the notice of the aggrieved party, the Conciliation Officer informs the other party that the procedure could be started. The Conciliation proceeding is supposed to be completed within the 60 days but it can be extended to a few days more on the request of the parties on writing form but the extension cannot be done beyond six months. The procedure ends when the settlement is signed or failure report is submitted by the officer to the government. If the government feels it to refer to the labour court, it provides sufficient reasons for the same including the time limit for disposal of the case. In case of individual worker, the court must decide the case within a period of three months.

In case of individual worker, for the state of West Bengal, for example, he can directly approach the labour court. When the dispute of the worker could not be decided by the Conciliation Officer, then after receiving the certificate from the officer the worker can apply labour court. The court is supposed to decide the case within 60 days. But in case of collective dispute nobody can approach the court except on the recommendation of the concerned government. But this can be done if both the parties agree and apply to government for the same and it can be refered to court. The judgement of the court is known as Award which is to be implemented within 30 days and it is binding on both the parties. Also in cases concerning the dismissal and retrenchment of a workman, the case is to be decided within sixty days. After that if either of the parties is not satisfied, it may file case in High Court or Supreme Court. If the party is employer than the full wages is to be given to the workers till the case is decided.

Besides the above mentioned method, there is another method to settle the dispute, *i.e.*, voluntary arbitration method. Here in this method, both the parties can opt an independent person as mediator for their case. In this case, the decision must be taken before the government refer the case to the labour court. The decision of arbitrator is final and binding to both the parties as there is no appeal court against the decision.

Strikes and Lockouts

Whenever a group of workers, on the basis of common understanding refuse to work, it is called strike. The strike is the ultimate weapon of the workers to fight to acquire justice from the employer. In order to give legal sanctity to the strike, certain points are to be taken into consideration. They are for example, the strike is to be legal, justified and rational. To say a strike legal, a few further points are to be noted. While conciliation is going on, no strike is to be taken place, while adjudication is in progress, no strike is to be taken place and while arbitration is going on, no strike is to be taken place.

If it is justified, then a strike can be done. But if court has upheld a strike which is not motivated by demands unconnected with the workers grievances, not unnecessarily prolonged and there is no violence or damage of property. It is therefore to be noted by the workers that the wages of the workers are to be paid by the employer if the strike is legal. A strike or lockout is illegal when the court gives verdict against the strike or lockout.

Lay-off

Lay-off means the temporary inhability, failure or refusal of the employer to the workers for their employment due to some problems in the industry not due to the workers but due to other reasons. Lay-off does not mean discharge from the service. The employment relationship continues between the employer and workers during the period. During this period, a lay-off compensation is to be paid to the workers as they are not responsible for lay-off period. However, for the compensation, there are variations in three types of industries as (*a*) industry employing less than 50 workers, (*b*) industry where there are more than 50 workers and (*c*) there are industries numbering more than 50 to 100 workers or more. For the first type of industry, full wages to be given, for second type of industry, 50.0% of the wages is to be given and for third type of industry, the workers are entitled for 50.0% of basic wage and dearness allowances. But in order to get this compensations, workers have to be ready to work in other units of the industry at the radious of five kilometers, the workers are to be present at the work place at least once in a day, if the lay-off continues more than one week, then at least once in a week, the workers are not suppose to work in other places, workers must have worked at least one year continuously. But if the lay-off done by means of go-slow by the workers then no lay-off compensation is given. The act states that the lay-off compensation stops after 45 days. The employer must take permission from the government before taking the lay off period especially in those industries where there are more than 100 employees. The workers are also to be informed regarding lay-off period by the employer.

Retrenchment

Retrenchment means termination of service of an employee by the employer for any reason except the termination due to punishment, retirement on supernnuation, voluntary retirement and termination due to ill health. In case of retrenchment of a workers, 15 days average pay for each year of service completed by the worker is to be given. While retrenching the workers, the employer must follow the principle of "last come first go".

Secondly, the employer must give one month notice to the concerned workers to be retrenched with specific reasons thereof, payment of compensation and finally he must inform the government, while in those establishments where there are more than 100 workers the employer must give three months notice, three months pay, seek prior permission from the government, specific reasons for such retrenchment.

Closures

In order to close the industry, the employer has to fulfil certain conditions as in case of industry which has less than 50 workers the employer must give one month notice while in case of industry having more than 50 workers but less than 100 workers, the employer has to give one month notice to the workers and two months notice to the government with specific reasons. In case of industry having more than 100 workers, the employer has to apply to the government of the closure before 90 days. It is to be noted that a unit can not be closed without the permission of the government. The rules of compensation is same as in case of the retrenchment. If an industry which was closed for sometime and it is going to reopen then the preference is to be given to the workers who were working there before its closure. If the employer does not follow such rules than he will be punished with Rs. 5000 as fine and imprisonment upto six months or both. This is for the industry owner who has more than 100 workers while the employer who has less than 100 workers, the punishment is Rs. 100 or one month imprisonment or both.

Payment of Gratuity Act, 1972

The gratuity is given to the employee in cash at the time of retirement. It is not a charity or alms but a legal right to the worker. The act was twice ammended in 1984 and 1987. The gratuity is given to the worker who has completed at least five years of service and in each year he has to do 240 days work. The act states that the worker will get 15 days wages for each year of service. The calculation of fifteen days wages will be based on the last pay drawn by the worker before his or her retirement or resignation. However, there is a bit difference in calculation of daily rated and monthly rated workers. For a monthly rated worker it is the last pay drawn × number of years of service × 15 days and then divided by 26 days. For daily rated worker, it is daily wages for three months × number of years of service × 15 days.

But it is to be noted that the gratuity may be forfeited if the worker has damaged the poverty of the industry. If damage is done then the amount of damage will be deducted from the gratuity payable to worker, or worker's service has been terminated due to misconduct. But the employer can not deduct from the gratuity any loan taken in the past at the time of retirement. In order to get the gratuity, the worker immediately after his or her retirement or retrenchment should apply in Form No. 1 of the Gratuity Act, 1972 which is available to the employer or the worker can get the form from the labour department of government (Assistant Labour Commissioner). After receiving the form duly filled up, the employer calculates the amount of gratuity to be paid to the worker and the worker has to be informed accordingly as also an intimation is to be given to ALC. The employer is bound to pay the gratuity within 30 days of the issue of notice in Form No. 1. If he does not do so then he has to pay simple interest to the worker at the rate of ten percent per annum.

The calculated amount may be challenged by the worker in relation to the years of service, number of days of payment etc. In such cases the worker can appeal to ALC to check the facts. In such case the employer has to deposit amount to the appropriate authority. Even if the son or daughter of the plantation worker is given service, the gratuity must be given to the retiring worker. This is relevant in plantation industry where there is a system of Badli job to the worker's son or daughter. If on this ground, the employer does not pay the gratuity then the worker can apply to ALC on Form No. 2 of the act. The ALC if after his persuasion with the employer, can not realise the gratuity then in this case, the ALC will inform the district Magistrate who recovers the amount from the employer's property. If the worker dies then his/her nominee will get the gratuity. The nominee may be wife or husband or married or unmarried children and dependent parents if there is no children.

Employees Provident Fund Act, 1952

This is another act like gratuity to provide some security to a worker after his or her retirement. But unlike gratuity, PF is created after collecting the contributions of workers and employer and it is consider that the workers must have greater right to enjoy the fund in times of need even at the time of working in the industry. Actually, it is a kind of saving of the workers. The workers in tea plantations must realise the significance of the fund as it serves as a source of security. They must see that their money for PF is properly deposited in the office of Provident Fund Commissioner. We have to stress this aspect as normally it is noted that often the money is not deposited in time by the employer of tea plantations. If this happens then the workers must report to the office of Provident Fund Commissioner so that legal action may be taken in time. Therefore, the workers must note that the PF is not a charity given by the employer but a right given by the government. The act is valid throughout the country except Jammu and Kashmir. The main objective of the act is to ensure that workers must have something for their retired life. This act is applicable to all the plantations of the country except where there are less than 20 workers. It means that it is valid in those plantations where the provisions of Plantation Labour Act, 1951 are applied. The act applies to a worker when he or she joins tea plantation and then only he or she is to be made the member of the PF scheme of the government.

Section 6 of the act states that the PF is made up of contributions from the employer and employees. The worker will contribute eight and one-third percent of his or her wages to the fund every month and the employer will make the amount deposited. It must be noted that the wage constitutes the cash wage given to the worker as well as cash equivalent of food concessions (ration) given. The amount eight and one-third percent of the wage actually means the one month's wage in a year. Hence, the worker must know that total amount of his or her PF in each year is one month's wage from his contribution and one month's wage from the employer. Therefore, one year PF means two month's wage of his or her monthly salary. This along with the contribution of the employer is to be deposited to the office of PF organisation which is managed by the Central Government which gives 8.0% interest per annum.

The worker can withdraw total amount of the fund on the following conditions:– Firstly, any worker who retires at the age of 55 years due to ill health, mental reason, T.B. leprosy or cancer. Secondly, on termination due to retrenchment or on voluntary retirement, discharge etc. Thirdly, on leaving the job due to shifting to some other job, leaving the country etc. Unlike in the past, now the employer can not withheld the contribution towards the fund from his share. This is done by amendment in 1990.

Suppose a worker dies before his retirement, then his/her nominee or nominees if there is more than one person, can draw the fund. Again, if a person or worker wants advance during his or her service period, it can be given for certain specific reasons such as buying dwelling land (Para 68 B) provided he or she has deposited more than Rs. 1,000, illness, marriage or education of children. The amount or loan will be realised by the employer within 36 installments. However, in case of education and marriage of the children, fifty percent of deposited amount can be withdrawn. But, to get the loans from PF, certain conditions are to be fulfilled. Firstly, the worker must be the member of PF scheme at least seven years and not more than three advances can be taken for the same purpose. Secondly, it is possible for a worker to pay for premium on his or her life insurance policy through his or her PF contribution. But the worker must inform the employer about this and necessary amount can be deposited from the PF contribution. Thirdly, in case of closure or lookout, she or he can get the advances. The para 68B of the act states that if there is a lookout for fifteen days or more than the worker can be paid the advance in toto. In case of the lockout or closure is for more than six months the worker can withdraw in addition to the total amount of his or her contribution the employer's contribution as well. According to the para 68B, any lockout or closure whether it is legal or not is considered as closure. If in case of discharge of a worker or dismissal from the work, then he or she can draw upto half of his or her contribution. This is so as the worker can feed up his or her family till a new job is found.

To get the PF, an individual or worker has to apply in Form No. 19 which is available with the employer. If in case of death of a worker, his or her nominee has to apply in Form

No. 20. The filled up Form has to send to nearby PF office after getting attestation of the Form by magistrate, gazetted officer, post-master, Gram Panchayat member or Pradhan, Chairman of Municipal Committee or Zilla Parisad, office bearers of registered trade unions and similar officers. The PF officer if feels doubt in any point can verify the same. The employer if fails to deduct contribution from the worker's side then he has to deposit the Provident Fund deductions from the worker's wages and his own contributions with the Provident Fund authorities, then he will be liable to be punished under section 14 of the Act and also under section 405, 406 and 409 of the Indian Penal Code. This means that the employer will be charged with misappropriation and criminal breach of trust. Both these actions involve heavy punishment which can lead to jail upto five years and fine and both.

Since 1995, 16th November, the Provident Fund has started the Pension scheme for the workers under the PF Act. As per the pension scheme, 8.33% of the contribution of the employer is to be deposited for the pension scheme of the workers. The pension is fixed at the time of retirement of the workers. However, the workers are to note the point that pension is fixed on the basis of average wages of the workers paid during the last year of the service. For instance, if a worker in his or her last year of service drawn Rs. 72,00 then the pension will be fixed at Rs. 600 per month. But if another worker has drawn only say Rs. 6000 during the year then his or her pension will be fixed at Rs. 500 only. To get full pension benefit, the workers are to work in all the days of work in the tea plantations so that maximum pension can be drawn for the retired life. Once the pension is fixed no change can be done later on. This is very important for the workers as absenteeism is very big problem in the tea plantations among the workers specially after they get wages and bonus and other payments from the plantations. The pension can be dawn by his or her dependents or nominee (*s*) if she or he dies. If the dead worker is male then his wife can daw the pension at the rate of 50.0% of the amount as used to draw by her husband and vice versa if the dead person is female. Again, if there is no wife or husband then the pension can be drawn by the children at the rate 25.0% till the children are at the age of 25 years. But it is not so in case of the worker himself or herself, even then he or she will be getting the same if alive till 80 years of age. Suppose a retired worker is living in the age of 80 years, even then he or she will be eligible for the pension. It means for the retired worker the pension will be paid till his or her death. It is the duty of employer to get ready with all the relevant papers relating to pension of a worker before he or she retires and send the same to the Provident Fund Office. The pension is to be given to the workers within one month of their retirement.

4

Introductory on Impacts of Globalization

The introduction of tea industry in India was ipso facto a by-product of British globalization process ever since 1831 when the British Government did not get the tea products from the Chinese companies. To meet the tea crisis in London, Lord William Bentick, the then Governor-General of India, appointed an expert committee to explore the appropriate tea growing zones in the country (Sharma and Das : 2008). The expert Committee recommended the following areas for introducing the tea plantations :

1. The lower hills and valleys of the Himalayan range;
2. The Eastern Himalayas/North Eastern Frontiers of British India;
3. The Nilgiris (South India).

Prior to that, one Shri Robert Bruce found that the tea plant was very common among the Singhpoo tribes of Changlang district of Arunachal Pradesh of North-East India since their immigration to Assam from Burma (Maynmar). In order to procure tea seeds and plants, he entered into an agreement with Bom Bisa Gamm, the tribal chief of Singpoos and supplied tea seeds and plants to Kumaon hills, Darjeeling hills, Terai, Dooars and Assam (Deb : 2007). In the process, the Chabua tea estate (Dibrugargh) district of Assam) was established in 1833. In Darjeeling, Dr. Campbell, the then Superintendent of British Government for Darjeeling, started a tea plantation at Allobari in 1840. In Terai belt of Darjeeling district of West Bengal, the tea cultivation started in 1864 and in Dooars areas of Jalpaiguri district of West Bengal, it was started in 1874. In 1916, the Maharaja of Tripura started tea plantations in the state of Tripura.

The spectacular feature of tea industry was that the planters sent from London pursued the tea projects (Sharma: 2000) on an experimental basis. So, in the beginning, the industry had no permanent objective as such. That was adequately supported by the fact that the British tea products were to be established on globalised basis to earn the global image for the then British Government. Considering the non-participation of the local people in the plantation pursuits, the British planters started importing the workers (Bhowmik: 1981) from various parts of the country and even from Nepal, Sikkim and Bhutan. Therefore, the workers were recruited following all sorts of dubious methods and treated them as temporary coolies to be tamed till the plantations would remain viable. This is evident from the terms and conditions of recruitment of tea plantation workers and their employment in which coercion, low wages, isolation, indenture (Bhowmik: 1995) and captivity were the obvious techniques for taming the illiterate coolies. Meeting the shortage of labour in the plantations, the planters used to employ the married couples *i.e.,* male, female along with their children. So, nothing unusual caused due to the running away of the workers from the plantations. Thus, nothing except the casualisation of tea garden universe was the characteristic feature of the plantation industry ever since its formative period. The workers who were unmarried were forcefully married on the way from their places of origin to the plantation enclaves. With the increase of demography in the plantations, the planters started Hatta Bahira system in Darjeeling tea gardens. The Hatta Bahira means the workers were ousted from the plantations stating or blaming them for their small mistakes commited at the plantations like indescipline, resorting to unionisation, seeking welfare benefits etc. To capture the global market with sufficient profit, the planters used to provide very low wages without extending any other facility as of an industrial society to the workers even upto the eve of independence of the country in 1947. However, after the independence of the country and influx of trade union organisations after 1950 (Bhowmik : 1996) being officially supported by the then political parties and government, the planters started to pay low wages on piece rate basis in high plucking season of the year. In this way, the casualisation of tea plantation workers started as normal course of labour employment and it has coined new dimension today in the period of transition of the industry as duly brought about by the Liberalisation, Privatisation and Globalization policy of the government. It shows that the so-called "Downsizing the Work Force" as started after 1991 in other technologically most sophisticated industries of the country has also logically well structured giving absolute rationality as a gerneric fact that is obviously accredited for the survival of industries in the competitive era. Thus, the casualisation is rather a legacy followed by the present planters/owners and to a great extent it has become more pragmatic approach suitable to the "Enclave" nature of tea plantation industry in the country.

Another notable feature of tea plantation industry ever since the days of British planters under the process of linking tea industry to the global economy was the employment of more and more female workers in the industry. Therefore, the feminisation as structured nicely today by the Globalization process was already there in the plantation industry in a rudimentary form. This may be the apparent reason why today there are more than fifty percent of female tea plantation workers in tea industry along with ninety percent of female casual workers in the Eastern Himalayas including Darjeeling hills. Most of the male workers are either supervisory staffs or office Babus or factory workers (Sharma: 2000). The employment of more and more females as workers has been supplemented by the British legacy that has stated that the finger tips of females are very sensitive to pluck the qualitative tea leaves followed by their sincerity to duty as well as their love, affection and tender care that they put on to the tea bushes and leaves as they do in case of their own children (Sharma: 2005). Moreover, due to their double roles that they tender (Bhadra: 1997) as worker and housewife, they are little inclined to the unionisation process which the tea garden management do not want to see by heart and soul as they want to rule the plantations with their unilateral decisions because still they believe the plantations as their "Plantocracy" established by themselves (Devi : 1989). This may be the background reason why in the Eastern Himalayan tea industry, male folks prefer the outside jobs. Of course, this has helped the female folks of the plantations to lead better quality of life with the money being sent by their male counerpart from the outside jobs. It shows that the plantation workers of the region under study do not at all completely depend on the plantation economy for their livelihood. This had been sufficiently translated by the ground reality with the abandonment of Pashok, Via Tukvar, Puttong, Samabong and other tea estates of Darjeeling hills which were mainly under the ownership, management and Control of Tea Trading Corporation of India Ltd. as well as the West Bengal Tea Development Corporation Ltd. Rather, the workers through their Self Managed Cooperatives could earn better income during the period of closure as most of the workers have built Puccka houses of their own and also purchased vehicles. Managing the closed/abandoned tea plantations, the workers gained sufficient confidence and understood the importance of Human Resources of the plantations as they became the direct stake holders of the same.

Present Phase of Tea Garden Globalization

With the withdrawal of Sterling companies and other multinational enterprises from the tea frontiers due to Foreign Exchange Regulation Act (FERA) of 1973 which did not allow the multinational companies to expand or diversify their industries, the plantations started transfering into the hands of Indian owners especially after 1991. Again, the Indian companies later on after 2000 A.D., also started escalating the tea front from investing their money so earned from the tea industry. After 2000 A.D., the tea garden owners started to invest their money to other sectors of Indian economy as per the provisions of the globalization policy of Government of India. This has caused for dwindling the tea industry in absolute sense of the term. This is evident from the dramas recently played by trade unions, management, government and other organisations in regard to the closed tea gardens of Darjeeling and Dooars regions of West Bengal ever since the last one decade or so of their closure/ abandonment. Rather, now they have come up with whimsical alternatives known as 'Informalisation' of tea industry so as to shift its status from formal to informal sector, in the light of globalization of Indian economy. It indicates that the tea gardens are to be managed by Self Help Groups or workers cooperatives by providing little financial supports from the outside agencies. This means that workers self managed tea estates is the only viable option left out as per the solution articulated by them today in the period of globalization and here in this context, the Government of West Bengal has opted Tea Tourism taking 5.0% of vacant tea garden land to solve the problems of tea plantations through outside agencies. It is evident from the observation made by the Labour Committee for Second Labour Commission in 2001. It is observed that the impacts of globalization had been viewed by the Labour Committee on 14.2.2001 in the following manner:—

1. Although concern was expressed by the committee that globalization will have a negative impact on employment and that it will not improve the condition of the poor, by and large the consensus (aimed at among tripartite members) was that we can not escape competition as a process. We can only think of following right policies to tackle the forces

of globalization and reap its positive benefits on growth and employment. We should also try to mitigate the negative impacts of globalization.

2. There is a need to focus on skill development and human resource development and skill upgradation on a sustainable basis.
3. There is a need for improving the work culture of all stake holders which will be conducive for quality and productivity. In the face of international competition, the culture of productivity is of utmost importance.
4. Employment generation with adequate social protection is a priority area while adderssing issues on globalization.
5. Labour can not be treated as a commodity. The human aspects of globalization are of highest concern and quality of life of workers must receive adequate attention from all social partners.
6. While gearing itself for global competition, the need to maintain social cohesion should not be lost sight of by industry.
7. There is a need for review of labour laws in order to adequately address the challenges confronting both industry and labour.
8. It was agreed that an updated note on impact of globalization on employment will be brought up for discussion in ILO forums.

Today, under the process of globalization, the tea garden owners are given free hand to lockout the plantations and invest the money so earned from the plantations elsewhere the country or outside. The Indian Tata group of industries has already started more than fifty tea estates in Sri Lanka. Stating the reasons for leaving the Indian tea frontiers, the owners of the plantations stated that no more tea industry comes under the purview of "Competitive or Productive

Enterprise" that has really been able to compete the global tea producers. Further, they stated that the politics of plantation trade unions do not at all allow for the establishment of pro-rata system, i.e., payment of wages and other incentives according to the quantum of work done by the workers in the industry along with the denial of trade unions to give stress on "Wage-Productivity Nexus" of globalized economy. Problem of cutting the cost of production is another reason why they are leaving the industry. It is due to high social commitments as per the provisions of Indian labour legislations ever enacted in relation to the welfare or fringe benefits of the workers. This has been merely accentuated by the system of making organised sector tea products at low cost because the global buyers want high quality tea at low cost. So, "High Quality-low Cost Nexus" of globalization makes the traditional tea industry sick like other sick indusries of the country. Tea plantation also comes under the purview of a social system (Bhowmik: 1981) which has many social clauses to be met by capital (Ratnam : 2004) for workers as human resource capital who are agro-based by occupation having low level of education and technological expertise (skill). To the owners, the plantation workers have become unproductive human stocks to meet their global demands. This is glaringly cited in the report of Second National Labour Commission (NCL) in 2001. In a sentence, NLC cited the process 'to cut short the rights of the workers at the organised industries' including the plantations. This is the cardinal feature of the NCL report. On other hand, NCL report has given free hands to the owners in declaring lockouts when it deemed fit without giving the same right to the workers to declare strikes as per the provisions of Industrial Disputes Act, 1947. Instead, the government is undermining those strikes which do not have the support of 51.0% of workers of the organised industries. This leads to the breakdown of trade union movement as well as the lossening of trade union recognition. Any kind of fissiparous tendency of the workers such as go-slow, pen down strike, misconduct etc. are considered as 'Social Evils" of the organised sector workers by the government. So, this sort of denied rights as provided by Industrial Disputes Act, 1947 (Govt. of India : 1947) constitute the social obligations of the workers in the present era of globalization. This may be the reason why now the trade unions are trailing ahead with its labour movement in defensive way rather than offensive manner as they used to do prior to 1991 when trade unions were called as militant organisations of the workers. In many cases, now good many early tea planters/producers have become distributors by collaborating themselves with multinational tea distribution agencies like Tata tea with Teetley or Gooderick or Duncan or Earl Grey etc.

Today, with the casualisation of tea plantation workers, a class of labour contractors has been emerged among the trade union leaders of the plantations to earn money out of the way. In one way, they have become the 'parasites' of tea garden working class. This has made the workers absolute serfs. Under, the cost cutting competitive edge as ordained by the globalization process, the management have formed important linkage with the contractors who help the management in different ways such as reducing cost for searching casual workers, reduction in welfare expenditure, cheap labours, reduction in power of trade unions, curtailment of medical and other facilities. In this way, the permanent work force has been un-bundled into casual labour stocks who are at their liberty to work as "right-less" workers of tea industry. This may be one of the reasons for decreasing trade union membership as rank and file workers understood that their trade union leaders are being secretly appointed as labour contractors by the management of the industry. In fact, it has helped the management to increase their profit margin even if some money is to be given to the labour contractors of the industry. This "Contractors-Management Nexus" has made the workers super-exploited today although they were under the organised exploitation system till 1991 as they were partly exploited by trade unions, partly exploited by the management and again partly exploited by the government agencies (Sharma : 2008). Therefore, "Serfdom" or "Serfhood" or "Super-Exploitation" is the characteristic feature of tea plantation workers today. It indicates the state of socio-economic agony of the plantation workers. The agony is increasing day by day. In the name of human resource development among the workers, the planters are pursuing some stray training programmes half heartedly for the sake of making their manpower resources capable over-night to compete the global tea producers under the forces of global competition so that they can easily connect the tea industry with the global market. Under the process, the "Fight or Flight" alternative of globalization appears to be the only viable option left out to the owners of the industry.

However, to relieve the industry from the point of view of cost effectiveness (Asopa: 2004) of production, the government has started introducing Panchayati Raj institutions in the industry with an idea to share the cost of production of the industry by providing certain welfare incentives to the workers like health facility, education facility to the children of the workers upto primary level, transport-communication connections and creating jobs under the various self employment schemes of the government. It is reported by some management personnel that the industry is relieved with 30.0% expenditure cut under the welfare facilities given to the workers from the Panchyati Raj institutions of government. For example, providing 100 days work under the National Rural Employment Guarantee Act, 2005 of government of India to the unemployed youths has helped the industry to a great extent especially solving the problems of non-workers of the industry.

In spite of this, under the philosophy of Fight or Flight, what is happening today is the flight of tea garden owners from the industry. It is evident from the non-payment of

Rs. 377/- crores (Tea Despatch : 2008) under the Provident Fund and Gratuity acts of the government to the retired and on the job wokers of closed/abandoned tea gardens of North Bengal. Though the Government of West Bengal has ownership of most of the tea gardens, which are closed down for more than one decade, not much has been done so for to terminate or cancel the lease agreements of the owners of the industry as per the provisions of FERA. It means that practically the workers are left alone to hell in the globalization process of government resulting which the workers are fully under illusion with all sorts of agonies. In fact, the owners are not paying dues, pretending that they have not closed down but abandoned the gardens for the time being. In reality, they are absconding the plantations for ever. Today, the agonies of the workers are not that apparent to look at while in the past they were under the process of agonising by the management overtly. This is apparent from the fact that hardly in the histroy of tea industry, the planters ever trust the workers rather they used to think and behave them as "illiterate coolies" of manual type of the agro-based industry possessing very low level of education, skill and expertise.

Tea Industry under Crisis

The tea industry earned Rs. 2130.73 crores of rupees in 2007 to the national exchequer. The tea production has increased to the tune of 250 times since independence of the country. This is the bare reality why the government is still trying, of course very casually, to articulate some steps for managing the industry as it is a national image making enterprise. However, the government has not been able to sort out solution to improvise the industry properly because the fifteen tea estates are still closed down in Dooars region of Jalpaiguri district of West Bengal. This is the reason why some national trade union leaders stated that there appears to be a death of Working Class, Emergence of New Proletarians etc. etc. for the workers who are forced to shift their loyalty towards oblivions. The culture of compromise and utter surrender are the present way of living of workers no matter whether it is very much unrealistic or mechanical because they have to meet their daily essentialization at homes in the absolute sense of the term.

The plantation workers as human resources are no more considered as crucial economic unit or factor of production. Due to the "End of Work", they have been plying under the "Social Exclusion" process. Rather, they are considered as "Social Dumping" as widely categorised under "Flexibilisation" process of labour force. By "Flexibilisation of labour force", globalization unleashes the following:—

1. External Numerical Flexibility—number of workers adjusted in accordance with the needs of management:
2. Internal Work Flexibility—working hours adjusted according to the needs of the management;
3. Externalisation-part of works of tea industry is put out through the outside contractors;
4. Functional Flexibility—workers jobs modified according to the needs of management;
5. Wage Flexibility—workers rewards (wages) as per the pro-rata system-Labour-Productivity-Market Conditions-Nexus;
6. End of Labour Welfare measures with trade union and government high patronage to the management of the industry.

A pertinent question arises is really the globlization has affected or impacted the working class of tea industry or not. Conceptually, what has happened is the cent percent of tea plantation workers of the region have not so far heard anything about the name called the "Globalization". Neither any one else has so far made them understood about the meaning, concept and implications of golobalization. In fact, for the workers, the Mela (field jobs) and domestic chores form the intergral part of their tea plantation life. The agrarian nature of plantation economy along with agrarian pursuits at homes after their tea garden jobs or duty hardly makes any difference in so far as the impacts left by the globalization of tea industry is concerned, So, the globalization issue appears to be the 'Hot Cake' for the tea garden management and owners. Had it really a damaging nomenclatura, then the workers may have made it an urgent issue to be addressed to the management in the gardens. In fact, it is the tea plantation management and owners who are clinging to make the industry sick during the last seventeen years of globalization ever since 1991. The issue is coining their days. In spite of management claim about the damaging impacts of globalization to the industry, why the owners are continuing their ownership of the industry is a big question being asked by the workers of the industry. What in fact, challenging the industry is due to the non-transparent legacy of the management towards the workers in regard to the blending of Darjeeling orthodox tea that has been fetching low prices in the market. The ten million kilograms of made tea of Darjeeling tea plantations has been blended into forty million kilograms. This is the source of blemishness for Darjeeling tea industry. Further, the trade logo meant for Darjeeling orthodox variety of tea has been whimsically administered to all the orthodox producers of the country and even Sri Lanka. This has of course, lately accepted by all concerned as the responsible factor for the annoyance of foreign buyers of Darjeeling orthodox tea. The local political parties also have a high ailment about the tea industry of Darjeeling hills. Rather, some of the top ranking trade union leaders stated that the industry is the colony of plainsmen in Darjeeling hills. The blood and sweats so poured by the workers throughout the last one hundered and fifty years of the history of Darjeeling tea industry, appear to be of secondary importance to the management and owners of the industry. This is clear in our understanding as most of the workers are women because the major percentage of male workers appears to be fully not committed to the industry because they think the tea garden jobs as the secondary source of their income being earned by their female folks. Hardly, any male worker apppears to be fully dependent on tea grden job as he is preoccupied with other non-plantation works. This is the reason why today the casualisation of female tea garden workers is increasing by leaps and bounds. Further, due to the sickness of industry thereby closure, abandonment, lockouts and work suspensions, the plantation workers are made more and more vulnerable as the plantation communities are treated as "Marginalised" communities of the region. Historically, the workers have shifted their living style from total deprivation as of the past to the total exit today in the industry. Asking the owners regarding the tea garden situation, they stated that they have not closed down the gardens but abandoned for the time being for which no closure notice is required to be given to the government as per the governance of globalization of Indian economy.

As stated above, the casualisation of female tea garden workers is increasing by leaps and bounds over the last one decade or so in the region. No more, tea industry is considered as "Green Gold" by the workers as they used to tell in the past with local proverb as 'Chiya Ko Bhot Ma Paisa Falcha' meaning thereby the tea bushes produce prompt money for the workers. Such "Social Exclusion" impact on the workers is the basic impression left by the forces of globalization of Indian tea industry in general and Darjeeling tea industry in particular. Any child having little bit educational qualification wants to leave the garden universe to urban areas of Darjeeling hills or outside. Observing and analysing the objective consequences of globalization in the Himalayan tea industry is the basic objective of present study. Everyone of the industry wants to move out in search of their better destiny. In fact, objective situation created by the globalization has both positive and negative impacts on the tea industry.

The Feminisation Process in Tea Industry

Altogether, 54.2% of workers are females in tea industry of the country. Considering the increasing level of expectation of the members of workers' families, the female folks of the plantations under study are joining more and more in number as casual workers which is locally known as Thicaka workers. This is simply due to the reactions of fear and insecurity unleashed by globalization process which has however on the other hand made the tea garden workers more and more settled with uncertainty and glow with culture of insecurity syndrome coupled with the generation of confidence for self development. This has on the other hand generated indirectly the competitiveness among the workers especially the male folks of the plantations in such a way that they have realised their utility as "Social Capital" in other sectors of the national economy. This is so because of the enclave nature of tea industry and trade union betrayals to the rank and file workers that have resulted into the wide mobility of tea garden males. The cosmopolitan nature of Nepalis has resulted into their mobility being shaped by their tradition to serve others giving tender care to the strangers as Maliks with smiling faces. This nature has attracted the global communities which in fact today seek their sincere services in the various sectors of global economy. It indicates the fact that globalization has encouraged the Nepalis of tea plantations to be mobile across the world. Their martial character (Northey and Morris: 1989) is being globally recognised. It is therefore a general perception that almost all the Nepalis of Darjeeling Himalayas want to go to foreign countries to work with all perseverance and earn sufficient money. This may be the apparent reason why the plantation workers do not at all scared of the consequences of closure of tea industry in Darjeeling hills. Even the Nepalis of Dooars region living and working in tea industry which were closed for the last fifteen years did not scared of the closure of the plantations as no Nepali has died of hunger so far in the Dooars closed tea gardens. This observation can be scientifically supplemented by the fact that no agitation was launched by any trade union or political party of the region stating the issue of the closed tea gardens of Darjeeling hills ever since 1991 to 2007. It shows that dependence on tea industry was supplementary ever since the introduction of Badli system by the British planters in Darjeeling tea industry which would abosrb only one child of a workers who retires from the tea plantation job. It is also because of the tradition of Nepali community which states that mostly a boy does not become a complete man unless he goes to unkown place and earns money. The Badli system does not make much difference in so far as the employment of children of the workers in the plantations is concerned as other children of the warkers do not get jobs in the plantations and hence they have to go out of the plantations. Once they go out, they do not want to come back to the plantations at least till they retire from the outside jobs. This is evident from the origin, growth and development of towns like Darjeeling, Kurseong, Mirik etc. where the people from the plantations have migrated and settled down for ever. It transpired the fact that a crude form of globalization was already there among the workers since the inception of tea industry in the region. Thus, in this respect, the globalization makes, remakes and refreshes the Neapli tea plantation workers in a new direction. Of course, the workers who are working in the plantations have generally to face "Serfdoom" as they are under the super-exploitation process in day today tea garden life. The planters are happy to make them serfs as they can tame them in whichever way they prefer with lesser wages that too are settled whimsically in industrial level agreements at the expiry of every three years at least theoretically. This is simply possible due to the existence of majority of female workers. Hence, the "Feminisation" process appears to be the workable philosophy that has over nicely comprehended by the tea planters and owners of the industry in regard to recruitment, employment and workers during the last two decades. The entry of majority of female work force has created a lot of implications in gender relationship in the households of the workers. Firstly, it has of course, helped them to limit their children structure upto a manageable level as the females also have to work for the household income. It has also generated a wide spectrum of contacts of women workers outside their homes. This is the obvious reason why today women workers are found to be very prominent in all the walks of life right from the kitchen garden to kitchen and from manual to technologically most sophisticated industrial jobs in the country. Many tea garden women workers have joined Self Help Groups in the neighbourhood under the ongoing women empowerment movement. Again, some of the women workers have opened shops of variety. These women workers of self help groups have also at times sharply attempted to deal with the cases of men's drukenness or alcoholism, physical abouse of wives and intervene the domestic disputes in favour of women of the plantation universe.

Secondly, while the impressions of some men in regard to women empowerment in relation to their engagement in tea plantation jobs are altogether different though they are eager to have some income from their women. Sometimes, some males fear of erosion of their authority or fear of sexual promiscuity of their women with other males because the women now have easy access to sterlization or other contraceptive techniques. Following this, some women workers told that they are being beaten by their husbands as they were to remain absent in the Mela (job) due to the side effects aroused following the contraceptive techinques. Thirdly, due to undergoing sterlization by wives, the husbands suspect their wives for sexual promiscuity with other males. It is because of the fact that they are free from the fear of pregnancy. However, the overall situation is that the women workers have earned emancipation from the traditional bondage of female domination of their husbands house.

Globalization and Labour in Tea Industry

The plantation workers stated that their owners simply pay their wages telling them that they have to work to get merely the wages. It implies the minimum wages only. No other entitlement as enshrined in the Indian labour legislations is guaranteed. The planters ask the workers not to demand for other rights in respect of Bonus, Gratuity, Family Pension, Provident Fund etc. This is the general platitude of plantation workers in North East India in general and Darjeeling hills in particular. The workers are found that under the situation they can not fight with the planters as their trade unions are favourably disposed of the management interests only. In this way, a kind of alienation is noticed among the workers towards the industry. Operating within the framework of a gradually liberalizing national economy, the government proved to be more and more supportive to industry than labour as the government policy has become more solicitous to capital or the owners of the plantations than labour in an attempt to attract the sustained industrial investment from the outside investors as well as the internal investors. Rather, the government has increasingly denounced the workers rights for their poor work culture and urged them to pull themselves up by tightening their feet straps for the industrial efficiency and competitiveness to make the region favourable to the investors. Now, the negotiated settlements with the owners is found to be the only option left to the trade unions for restoring harmonious industrial relations in tea industry. To the workers, it is a straight betrayal to the working class due to the reason that trade unions have done hasty agreements undermining the interests of the plantation workers. Therefore, the workers said that their trade union leaders are corrupt personnel of parasite type. The corruption is inter-connected with the casualisation of the plantation workers as trade union leaders have become labour contractors of the management of tea gardens. The management along with such dominant trade union leaders of corrupted type has combinedly launched the slogan that tea industry is a sick unit. While the rank and file tea plantation workers feel that it is a fabricated or created crisis by the vested interest group of the industry. In fact, there are various inherent factors responsible for the created crisis that include poor quality of tea leaves due to old bushes, their utter negligence in regard to garden maintenance (tea culture), constant change in regard to the ownership pattern, monopoly and cartelization of few buyers, monopoly of retailers and blenders. These factors influence prices to be fixed at the tea auction centres along with the contributions of small growers' sector to production, absence of value addition tea and other structural reasons that are garden specific. Violation of labour acts and basic livelihood rights of the workers are the open realities in tea industry. Otherwise, how the same workers who would earn good profit prior to 1991 became unproductive after 1991. Thus, some workers compare the vested interest people as Bin Ladens who are pretended to have become unreachable or unnoticeable to the government. Quite often, the workers stated their metaphors of having their hands and feet tied and being immoblized, their backbones being broken, lying prone to defeat, being beaten to abject submission, being down to their knees, dying and being dead, expecting mercy from the planters or otherwise wandering around, crying hopelessly for want of meagre bread and butter. Thus, the plantation workers feel themselves as hopeless and worthless creatures who have been tamed in colonial fashion as they are non-entities or the Kamanee Coolies in local Nepali language. The planters think that the workers are like donkeys, kick them more and then they will work more giving their all perseverance. This has generated different kind of violence in Darjeeling hill tea plantations. All the political movements including Gurkhaland movement have sprouted from the tea plantations in Darjeeling Himalaya. The Khati Khanee Manchees/Jati meaning thereby the hard working community that carries a rich legacy of the

Himalayas have become identityless "stock" today loitering in and out of the country in search of manual or other low graded jobs. Stating the political agitation in the region, the workers stated that they used to think the agitations in the past as the agitations of the Gurkha community as a whole but now the agitations are done for self interests of a few political leaders only. Thus, if they join the agitations whole heartedly as in the past, then they will be beaten to death while the political leaders will gallop away comfortably with the government patronage. It shows the reason for their attrition and assertiveness towards the leaders and industry. Therefore, the politics of trade unions is the nasty politics of a few leaders only today. Now, the workers have become cynical to the political parties and their approaches articulated so far in the region. Again, it is found among the youths that they are clinging to political parties and loitering here and there for no stable benefits except to fill in their pockets temporarily from such political leaders. Thus, the assasination of working class is found to be the outcome of globalization process among the workers of the Himalayan tea industry. It shows that there is no more efficacy of working class in tea industry.

Scope of the Study

Till today, there is hardly any empirical study on the impacts of globalisation among the tea plantation workers of Darjeeling Himalaya in the state of West Bengal. Majority of tea plantations were covered under the study. Except the work on the Tea Plantation Workers in the Eastern Himalayas by R.L. Sarkar and Mahendra P. Lama and the Himalayan Tea Plantation Workers by Khemraj Sharma, there is no other research study in the region. However, whatever the other studies have been done so far in the region, they are centered around production, productivity, market trends, sickness of the industry etc. So, this is a denovo attempt to study the impacts of globalization among the plantation workers of the Eastern Himalayas. The apparent significance of the study lies in the fact that globalization has both positive and negative impacts among the workers and industry of Darjeeling Himalayas.

Methodology of the Study

During 2006-07, an intensive field survey was done by the authors in Darjeeling Himalayan tea industry on the problem of study among the workers. There are about seventy tea estates with fifty two thousand workers in the Himalayan tea industry. Being the sons of the soil, we were able to get hold of the workers of the plantations although they were reluctant initially to cooperate us in our research venture. However, due to our long association with trade union leaders, management and political party leaders of the region, we could accomplished the work related to data collection in due time. We were also accessible to the workers as we belong to Central Board for Workers Education, under the Ministry of Labour and Employment, Government of India.

A mail questionnaire had been prepared carefully and administered the same to the trade union officials, management personnel and other non-Governmental organisations of the region. The collection of data was proceeded by our personal field work in the plantations of Darjeeling hills during 2006-07. The data were also collected from the secondary sources also such as Darjeeling Tea Association (Darjeeling), office of various trade unions, district library of Darjeeling, the Central Library of University of North Bengal (Darjeeling), office of Tea Board of India at Siliguri and Guwahati, and other offices of government like Gram Panchayats at the plantations in the region. Thus, the participant observation, interview schedule and field work form the basic methodology of data collection of the study. Finally, after collecting the data, both primary and secondary, the report writing was pursued on the problem of the study.

Studying the tangible impacts of globalization among the plantation workers, we will mainly focus on the socio-economic changes among the workers after 1991. Considering the fabricated sickness of tea industry, an introspective analysis has been done on the nature of casualisation of the Himalayan tea plantation workers and their exposure to outside the plantations due to globalization. Their traditional and modern health dimensions have also incorporated in the various chapters of the study. Some data on socio-economic changes are being compared with a study conducted by Khemraj Sharma in 2000 A.D. in Darjeeling Himalayan tea industry. The present study does not completely rely on the secondary data and theoretical sophistications or any other digressive approach ever adopted by many scholars on the Himalayan tea plantation industry and workers so far. The present study is therefore purely an empirical venture to study the tangible impacts of globalization among the tea plantation workers of Darjeeling hills with the data collected from tea estates of Darjeeling Himalayas of North-East India during 2006-2007.

5

Present Socio-Economic Conditions of the Workers

In this chapter, we shall see the socio-economic conditions of the workers in the era of globalization. Discussing their socio-economic conditions, we will concentrate on the structure of the workers, their family structure, mobility structure of the family members of the workers, types of houses of the workers, marriage patterns of the workers, land holding patterns of the workers, quality of life of the workers, socio-economic development of the workers, productivity and labour standards of the workers, health dimension of the workers etc. etc. The data have also been compared with another study conducted by Khemraj Sharma in 2000 A.D. in Darjeeling hills. Let us begin with the structure of tea plantation workers in Darjeeling Himalayas today.

The table No. 18 indicates that there were 47.7% of males and 52.3% females as permanent (Hazira) tea plantation workers in Darjeeling hills in 2000 A.D. Now, interestingly, the percentage of permanent male plantation has been decreased to 35.1% while the percentage of female permanent plantation workers has been increased from 52.3% to 64.9%. Again, there were 2,025 (66.3%) male and 1,025 (33.7%) female plantation workers of casual category (Thiccka) in 2000. A.D. Here too, the table portrays the fact that number of male casual workers has been decreased to 1,119, (5.7%) while the female casual workers has been increased to 18,638 (94.4%). It shows that the male folk do not give priority to tea plantation jobs as most of the male

Table 18. Tea Plantation Workers in Darjeeling Himalaya

Year	*Permanent Workers*			*Casual Workers Production*			*Production*	*Labour*
	Total	*Male*	*Female*	*Total*	*Male*	*Female*	*in Mil. Kg.*	*per hectare*
2000 A.D.	52,013	25228	27685	3053	2025	1025	12 Ml. Kg.	3.74
Percentage	—	47.7	52.3	—	66.3	33.7	—	—
2007 A.D.	47,106	16,494	30,602	19,757	1,119	18,638	10 Ml. Kg.	4.50
Percentage	—	35.1	64.9	—	5.7	94.4	—	—

Source: Sharma: 200; Field Work: 2007

folks have been engaged in other jobs either in the plantations or outside. The increasing percentage of casual tea garden workers has been closely associated with the feminisation as 94.4% of casual workers are females.

The observation indicates that the globalization of course with structural adjustment process of the industry, has been taken place in the composition of labour force. If it is so, then an obvious question emerges as to whether tea industry is really the backbone of plantation workers in Darjeeling hills or the people of Darjeeling hills. Another pertinent question is that how far it has sustained the socio-economic development of the workers. It shows that as elsewhere the country, the globalization has nothing to do with agriculture and agro-based industries. It is the matter of options for the workers alone to accept or not the tea garden jobs. The table clearly shows that only females have shown deep conviction towards the tea plantation jobs as 94.4% of casual workers (Thiċcka) are females. The land-man ratio has been tolerably increased by the management of the plantations to 4.50 per hectare in 2007 A.D. while it was at 3.74 per heactare in 2000 A.D. In fact, the increasing land-man ratio is the creation of tea garden management personnel who found it more profitable with the casual workers (Thiceka) who are simply paid their wages. Altogether, 16,704 casual workers have been recruited since 2000 A.D. while management decreased the permanent workers (Hazira) to the tune of 5,807 during the span of seven years. Thus, casualisation or contractualisation is being well received by the Himalayan tea industry. The casualisation with the termination of strikes by trade unions of the industry may be the apparent indication for resuming the closed tea gardens like Pashok and Via Tukvar tea estates of Darjeeling hills after their closure since the last sixteen years. The male mobility to non-plantation sectors of Indian economy has encouraged well for the casualisation of tea plantation workers in Darjeeling Himalaya. This is evident from the mobility structure of family members of the plantation workers in table No. 19 of the study.

Table 19. Workers and their Family Members (2007)

Sl.No.	*Total Households and the Workers staying in the plantations of Darjeeling Himalayas*	*Family Members staying within the hills and country*	*Family members staying in foreign Countries*
1.	(2,11,403 households)/66,063	1,32,126	13213
—	Percentage 31.2%	62.5%	6.3%

Source: Field Work: 2007

The table No.19 of the study transpired the fact that 31.2% of family members of the workers stay in the plantations while 62.5% of their family members are staying outside the plantations and still another 6.3% of their family members are staying in foreign countries. Thus, altogether 68.8% of the family members of the workers stay outside the plantations of Darjeeling Himalayas. The finding makes it clear that no more the tea industry is the backbone of the Himalayan plantation workers. Secondly, the 68.8% of the workers family members who are staying outside the plantations do obviously extend financial supports to the workers of the plantations. Therefore, it may be quite a realistic generalisation to draw from the above observation that tea industry may have carried national honour to the owners and management of the plantations and government of West Bengal and India under the present "Fight or Flight" alternative left by the globalisation process but it hardly matters much for the workers of the region for their socio-economic development. The globalization urges for global networking system which has rather helped the Nepalis of tea plantations of Darjeeling hills to move around the world as they have been liberalised from the traditional bondage system under Plantocracy (Devi: 1989). To be more specific, let us see the actual structure of family of the workers.

Table 20. Structure of Family in the Himalayan Tea Industry (2000 and 2007)

Year	*Joint*	*Percentage*	*Nuclear*	*Percentage*	*Total*
2000	7,293	17.5%	34,295	82.5%	41,588
2007	2,325	06.0%	36,617	94.0%	38,942

Source: Sharma: 2000, Field Work: 2007.

The table No. 20 of the study indicates that in 2000 A. D., 82.5% of family composition of the workers was of nuclear type consisting of husband, wife and children while in 2007 A.D., the percentage of nuclear family increased to 94.0%. It is found that only 6.0% of present family structure of the plantation workers is of joint type consisting of husband, wife, children, father, mother, father-in-law, mother-in-law and others while it was 17.5% in 2000 A.D. The geometrical increase of nuclear family today is due to globalization policy of Indian economy. Every body of the family wants to earn something and desires to lead an independent life in nuclear family. The nuclearisation of family structure is the concomitant outcome of globalization of tea industry in the region. Another pertinent factor responsible for the nuclearisation of family structure is due to the fact that compared to tea plantation workers of Dooars, Terai and Assam, the Nepali tea plantation workers are apparently literates who want to have complete independent living. The concept of independent living is more with the females than the males and as we have seen above that tea industry is fully under the feminisation process both conceptually as well as functionally and feminisation is a powerful force unleashed by the globalization of Indian economy. Females are not only endeavouring to manage the plantation jobs but also the homes along with other areas of socio-cultural peripheries of the society. They make all occasions beautiful, charming and well managed. Thus, female proficiency including their charmness as desired by the world customers make every moment more and more meaningful and pragmatic. The houses are also fully decorated and polished well by the women workers. This is evident from the structure of their houses.

Table 21. Typology of Workers Houses (2000 and 2007)

Year	*Kuccha*	*Percentage*	*Puccka*	*Percentage*	*Total*
2000	8,868	21.3%	32,720	78.7%	41,588
2007	4,312	9.5%	41,317	90.5%	45,629

Source: Sharma: 2000; Field Work: 2007.

If we make thorough analysis of the table No. 21 of the study, we find that in 2000 A.D., there was 78.7% of Puccka houses of the workers while 21.3% of their houses were of Kuccha type while in 2007 A.D., 90.5% of their houses are of Puccka type and only 9.5% of the same are of Kuccha type. The houses are made of wooden walls with corrugated iron sheet roofs. The size of Puccka houses are of 30″ by 20″ length and breadth respectively. Due to dercreasing number of family members, the existing houses are quite enough to accommodate the entire family members of the households. Secondly, due to the increase of expectation level of family members headed mainly by female workers, the female workers do not want the number of children who are unmanageable as they have to devote much of their times in tea garden duty and agrarian pursuits at homes. With the increasing popularity of computer and other means of information technology and education, each and every female worker wants to impart techincal and other higher education to their childeren. This has also helped to lower the birth rate among the workers in tea industry of the region especially during the last two decades. They send their children to schools and colleges for education and to have better performance even they opt tuition at Siliguri during the winter season when the winter holidays starts at Darjeeling hills. It needs substantial amount of money to be spent for completing the tuition package at Siliguri. This has also stimulated the female workers not to give brith to such number of children who are unmanageable at their end. Thus, it has generated a new dimension to their marital life today.

Table 22. Type of Marriage among the Workers

Year	*Intra-Caste*	*Percentage*	*Inter-Caste*	*Percentage*	*Total*
2000 A.D.	12,367	46.8%	14,086	53.2%	26,453
2007 A.D.	5,026	14.9%	28,737	85.1%	33,763

Source: Sharma: 2000; Field Work: 2007.

The table No.22 of the study indicates that in 2000 A.D., 46.8% of marriages of the workers had taken place within their respective castes and tribes while 53.2% of the same had taken place among different castes and tribes of the plantations while in 2007 A.D., only 14.9% of the marriages have taken place within their own castes and tribes and 85.1% of marriages have taken place among the various castes and tribes. Today, the percentage of love marriages is increasing at a faster rate as marrying couples want to have their sound economic position rather than sticking themselves to caste or tribal background. So, it is the economic background of marrying couples that mattters a lot today than the caste or tribal affiliations. The increasing inter-caste/tribal marriages is also due to the socio-economic situations of the region under study. In fact, every caste of Darjeeling Himalaya wants to be tribal today may be due to the reservation policy of government for the tribals in different government jobs and educational institutions. In 2005, Tamang and Limbu castes of Nepali community of the region got schedule tribe status. This is apparent from the demand for providing tribal status to Darjeeling hills by the Gurkha National Liberation Front (a regional political party) and Government of West Bengal as well as some other political parties of the region. Still other political parties are launching agitations demanding for Gurkhaland—the home land for more than one crore Gurkhas/Napalis of Indian origin.

Table 23. Workers and land holding patterns

Year	*Total land (in Acre)*	*In the Garden (in Acre)*	*Percentage*	*Outisde the Garden (in Acre)*	*Percentage*
2000 A.D.	996	364	36.5%	662	62.4%
2007 A.D.	1251	221	17.7%	1030	82.3%

Source: Sharma: 2000; Field Work: 2007.

The table No. 23 of the study shows that the land holding pattern of the workers has been changed because in 2000 A.D., the workers had 364 acres of kitchen land (Kothebari) in the plantations and 662 acres of land outside the plantations. In 2007 A.D., the question of land holding inside the plantations has been decreased to 221 acres only while the land holding pattern outside the plantations has been increased to 1030 acres. It indicates that tea plantation kitchen lands as given to the workers by the management of the plantations since the inception of industry has been converted into the tea planting area. Altogether, 82.3% of land holding of the workers is located outside the plantations. This may be another reason for decreasing interest of the workers towards the tea garden jobs. Normally, due to this, the tea garden workers remain busy in their outside land during the agrarian sowing and harvesting seasons. It is also found that some male workers left the plantations and engage themselves in other sectors of national economy for months together in an year. Interestingly, this has however encouraged the management to engage more and more female casual workers in the plantations. But it is also seen that nobody of the management personnel issues terminantion notice to such workers viewing the untoward consequences to be faced by the management later on from trade unions and political parties of the region. Again, it is also found that the management feel it needless as they are earning more and more profit since they do employ casual workers who are not to be paid any other fringe benefits except their normal wages. With the increase of trade and commerce in the region, many workers are found busy with their small shops giving secondary importance to tea garden jobs. Among the items of sale in the shops, alcohol is very common. Having such shops at their easy reach, the young generation, do not hesitate to drink alcohol in the shops. However, unlike in the past, Bhatti (liquer furnance) is no more found today in tea plantations of Darjeeling Himalaya. It is one facet of their quality of life in the plantations. Let us see the other facets of their quality of life.

Table 24. Quality of Life of the Workers

Year	*Vehicle*	*T.V.*	*Radio*	*Watch*	*Telephone Conection*	*Mobile Sets*	*Sofa Sets*	*Scooter/ Bike*
2000 A.D.	141	28,323	15,373	30,739	245	—	7.662	500
2007 A.D.	250	42,618	1200	32,766	105	25,687	10,668	3000

Source: Sharma: 2000; Field Work, 2007.

The table No. 24 of the study transpired the fact that the quality of life of the workers has been improved comparatively as indicated by the ownership of mobile sets of the workers in 2007 A.D. Interestingly, in 2000 A.D., no workers had mobile sets but now 25,687 mobile sets are being owned by the workers. The number of telephone connection has been decreased from 245 to 105 today. Again, increasing ownership of scooter/bike and vehicle indicates improvement in their quality of life. The infrastructural development and influx of international information technology through road-transport development, television and mobile sets have helped the workers also to improve their quality of life in the plantations. All the workers have now earned the knowledge about computer because they see the same in their garden offices resulting which all the workers want to impart computer education to their children. Some workers told us that tomorrow computer will totally replace the television sets and radio services. The changes are more comprehensible than apprehensible to the workers at home. Holding mobile sets is every body's status symbol of development today and they want to uplift their quality of life by owning the mobile sets. No more, they want to be backward "Kamanee Coolies" in the region as in the past.

The Informalisation of Tea Garden Universe

It is known from the study that workers of the plantations are purchasing more and more land outside the gardens which indicates the fact that informalisation of industry as brought about by the globalization has also affected the plantation frontiers of Darjeeling Himalaya. The term 'Informalisation' involves two things, viz, self-employment and secondly, emergence of more and more female work force in various sectors of economy. Tea plantation industry carries more and more informal characters as it is an agro-based industry with formal organisational herarchy from the skilled managers to manual (unskilled) workers. This may be the reason why tea industry has dual characteristics viz. agriculture and industry (Xaxa: 1997). It has manufacturing unit (Factory) along with agrarian specificities like field with tea bushes, paddy, maize, vegetables, oranges, Cardamom and animal husbandry ever since its inception. The only perceptible change taken place after the globalization is that the plantation sector has been introduced with uncertainty of works, workers and management following Fight or Flight philosophy in the competitive era. The other characteristic features as found today in tea plantations are uncertainty of employment, avoidance of labour laws and casualisation or contractualisation of work force. It shows that the very concept of "class" has been on the constant decay. This has made the workers to be defenseless, free and having absolute greediness. The informalisation as the process of change has been accredited by the government. The control over work process of the past by the workers has gone down today due to the decreasing role of trade unions in the industrial relation matters of the plantations. The informalisation of work force can thus be seen to proceed hand in hand with the feminisation of work force to tackle the poverty and backwardness of the plantations. The women in the process of informalisation provide a crucial link with the domestic economy and community in the process which has far reaching effects or impacts on the dynamics of plantation community of Darjeeling hills. Another dramatic change that is being taken place in the plantation industry today is the introduction of the concept of Tea Tourism taking 5.0% tea garden vacant land by the Government of West Bengal with an expenditure of Rs. 20 crores over the last few years but so for no tangible result has been evolved. In fact, the concept of Tea Tourism has been emerged in contradiction in so far as the socio-economic development project of the workers is concerned. Secondly, the Tea Tourism appears to be detrimental to eco-development of the fragile ecology of the Himalayas. Thus, how far the Tea Tourism will coined the day is an issue for future enquiry. Still another question is that how much we know about the spill-over effects of tea tourism among the plantation workers. In fact, the world famous tourist centre (Darjeeling) is polished with tea bushes as "Green Gold" ever quoted since the British days. Otherwise, the whole lot of beauty of the Queen of Hills (Darjeeling) will be finished into non-entity. Considering this, may be the half hearted efforts as being undertaken by the Government of West Bengal as well as the Government of India to continue the industry amids all sorts of lacunas committed for sustaining national image, will mostly be on papers only. Sustaining tea industry in the Himalayan niche is simply an image making drama of the government. Otherwise the Darjeeling Himalayan Railways, the receipient of world heritage status will loose its potency. The charmness that the tourists acord through their journey from Silliguri to Darjeeling will end if tea industry—the green gold zone is dwindle for ever. So, it is a national challenge for Government to end the tea industry in

Darjeeling Himalaya. If tea industry is closed down then it will be followed by the end of tourism industry for ever in Darjeeling because the snow tops of the great Kanchenjunga mountain shall deplete for ever. This is a kind of informalisation effect of globalization for sustaining tea industry in Darjeeling and not for the sake of development of people thereof alone.

The End of Potential Work Force

The absolute informalisation along with casualisation affects absolutely. The casual workers (Thiccka) who are borrowed from the neighbouring bustees or villages do not have deep commitments towards the tea industry and hence they work for the sake of doing work to earn more and more money which has affected the industry adversely. The informalisation process has been further strengthening by the introductioin of Panchayati Raj institutions in tea industry that has as reported by the management of tea industry helped them to reduce the cost of production to the tune of 30.0% at least theoretically on labour welfare head of the workers and unemployed youths under the National Rural Employment Guarantee Act, 2005 as non-workers problems as told by management is a big problem for the industry. The result is coarse plucking by the casual workers that has adversely affected the quality aspect of orthodox Darjeeling tea in the international market. The existing work force, of course, know the adverse consequences of coarse plucking but keep mum as their trade unions are apathetic to them. This is due to the emergence of trade union-management nexus which has beautified the informalisation process and hence the end of the importance of potential work force in tea industry of the region. This will in the long run affects the industrty in negative way. It indicates that tea garden workers as human resource, has no role to play in the so-called informalisation process of the industry because "labour" as the distinct class has been vanquished by the victorious consumerism or competitive capitalism as per the dictates of globalization policy of the government.

From the industrial relation point of view, the tea garden management used to be comprehended themselves not only the custodials of companies but also the guardians of the work force in the past. But today, they are simply the representatives of their owners (traders) of the industry. In this way, they own the industry fully but they have nothing to own the human resource (Sharma: 2008) i.e., the workers of the industry in so far as the socio-economic upliftment of the workers in the industry is concerned. Within the realm of "Fight or Flight" nexus of globalization, again, the industrial relation between the management and workers has become the relation of Neo-Master-Servant in nature. Making fool and foul to the working class following all sorts of filthy techniques with the patronage of trade unions and political party leaders appears to be the present nature of industrial relation in tea industry of the region. So, what is winning the day is not the capitalism in ideal sense but unique type of capitalist system of labour exploitation in an organised way of super exploited type.

However, to make a political mileage, the government of India as well as the Government of West Bengal through Shri Jairam Ramesh, the Union Commerce and Industry Minister stated in the recent international tea conclave at Guwahati (Assam) that special a plan protection fund has been earmarked in 11th Five Year Plan to save the sick tea plantations to the tune of two thousand crores. But the major conclave chunk of the fund went to South Indian tea estates including research and development works and hence only negligible amount (forty crores) has been sanctioned for the north Indian tea estates including North-East India. Another reason for this is that the owners and management of North Indian tea estates did not show keen interest to procure the fund at the appropriate time. The Darjeeling tea industry remains outside the zone of consideration for the same. In fact, it is due to the "Look East Policy" of government which has whimsically harps on erasing out the belligerent eyes of terrorist outfits towards the plantation sectors of North-East India including Darjeeling hills. It is because of the fact that no serious effort has been so far made by the government and owners of tea industry to stop "Brokers Raj" and "Blending Raj" for Darjeeling tea. This is supplemented by the fact that ten million kilograms of orthodox Darjeeling tea produced in 2007 has been blended into forty million kilograms. Secondly, the Darjeeling Tea Trade Logo has not been strictly maintained for Darjeeling orthodox tea only rather the same Logo is fully being utilised by all the orthodox producers of the country and even Sri Lanka, Nepal, Arunachal Pradesh, Sikkim etc.

Workers: The Subject of Blemishnesses for low Productivity

The tea garden management always blame labour for low productivity in tea plantations. In fact, industrial productivity is a generic term applicable to all the factors of production. How can the same work force have become unproductive after 1991 prior to which they were obviously the most productive force-is a big question today before the tea industry of the region. The other factors of production, viz., old tea bushes of more than one hundred and fifty years old, blending, constant changes in ownership pattern from the multinational companies to Inidan entreprenurship, Sahib-Coolie Raj, low labour standards etc. etc. have hardly brought under serious notice to the people concerned to address ever since 1947 to the globalized era as well as the negligence of government and trade unions. In fact, lack of vision is responsible factor for the sickness of tea industry today in the region. Thus, in reality, workers have nothing to blame for low productivity at least in the present era of globalization when their trade unions are defenseless organisations of the workers being purely coloured by political unionism which ultimately champions for management benefits in the light of globalization of the workers and industry by the government. This may be the apparent reason why today the management lockout the gardens in either pruning season or otherwise on issues like Provident Fund or Gratuity or Bonus payments of the workers following the Fight or Flight policy. What is the urgent need of the hour is that all the factors of production should be productive enough to address the global competition as the productivity destines to quality which is again an unending journey for all concerned factors of production. In fact, market as a new factor of production of the globalized era has been still neglected by the owners of the industry. This is supplemented by the low level of market survey and publicity pursued by the owners of the industry and Tea Board of India. Whatever the schemes on rejuvenation, uprooting of old tea bushes and gestation period are set forth by Tea Research Associations and Tea Board of India, they are mainly followed on papers only or they have been followed very very microscopically or at the low of level of compliance giving fake justification showing precarious financial condition of the industry. As the workers view that no tea garden is actually losing profit obsolutely in the globalized era, may be the profit margin has been decreased due to the global competition. This is due to the import of tea from Sri Lanka. Bangladesh and very very recently from Nepal as per the SAARC agreements (Bhowmik: 2008). The tea garden workers as marginalised work force of the country have nothing to do with publicity, monitoring and survey on the market situation.

The Tea Garden Workers: A Marginalised Work Force

Bhowmik (2008) observed that "tea industry is oldest manufacturing unit in the country that has employed more than one million work force. In other words, one out of seven workers of manufacturing sector is a tea plantation worker in the country. Despite their large numbers, the problems of tea plantation workers are often overlooked by those interested in labour studies because these workers are marginalised. They are isolated in their plantations, bound by low wages and poor working conditions. Their problems are rarely focussed in newspapers or journals nor discussed in workers forums. Neither the governments have given much importance to this section of working class of the country". Above all, the Himalayan tea plantation workers are super-marginalised since their problems are least heard even by the local state government and the mainstream trade union of Darjeeling Gurkha Hill Council (DGHC) in the truest sense of the term. The workers are agonised socio-economically as management give fake justifications among which the sickness is their cheap slogan today. But ever since the last one decade, internal customers to tea have been increased in the country along with the increase of production. This statement can be supplemented by 940 million kilograms of tea produced in the country in 2007 while in 2006, India produced 953 million kilogramas of tea. The established tea plantations along with small grower gardens altogether have increased tea production scenario of the country spectacularly today. With the declaration of Darjeeling Himalayan Railways as one of the world heritages has attracted the foreign customers and buyers for orthodox Darjeeling tea. This may be the reason why today ninety percent of Darjeeling tea is exported. Whenever any manager is asked about the export destination of his tea he states that his tea market is either in Germany or Japan or London or Afganistan or Pakistan or Iran. It shows that the potency of Darjeeling tea is still apparent to the foreign buyers. Thus, Darjeeling tea is not marginalised while tea making hands i.e., workers are rather super-marginalised in the globalized era. Hardly, the workers problmes are brought to the mainstream or natiohal policy framing platform. It is because of the fact that still hill tea plantation workers are branded whimsically by the mainstreams as immigrants or descendents of immigrants from Nepal, Sikkim and Bhutan Himalayas. This is the main reason why ever since 1917, there has taken place one agitation after another. For instance, today the Gurkha National Liberation Front has been replaced by Gurkha Janmukti Marcha under Shri Bimal Gurung. Otherwise, the world famous Darjeeling tea makers (workers) would have been on the top of world tea drinking dairy. The inherent agony of tea plantation workers is overlooked considering them as the peripheral community of mercenary type. There is no age bar for tea plantation jobs. They work till their physical status permits them to work for. Nowhere in tea garden job registers, their date of births are clearly mentioned so far. Thus, many workers are found dying on the job situation only. Very recently, new entrants among the workers are being entertained with their date of birth certificates. This may be one of the reasons for decreasing labour productivity of the garden workers.

The unhygenic labour lines (labour Dhuras) having no drainage system, has affected their health due to polluted water coming from the streams or Jhoras where there is dirty water reserviours coming down from one labour line to another. However, it is also found that hookworms and tuberculosis are common diseases today among the tea plantation workers of Darjeeling hills. Recently, more than one hundered HIV Aids patients are found in tea plantations of the region. One of the reasons for the spread of HIV Aids in the plantations is due to the disease being brought by the working males outside the plantations in some big cities. This has also multiplied the agony of the workers. Lack of good health services of the management system is responsible factor for the spread of other diseases including tuberculosis among the workers. The agony of tea plantation workers belonging to marginalised community for the national mainstreams is well supplemented by the killing of tea garden tribal workers in November, 2007 in Guwahati (Assam) when they were claiming for their tribal status in

Assam. Similarly. step-motherly treatment of government of West Bengal had been done to the tea plantation workers of Darjeeling hills during Gurkhaland agitation (1984 to 1988) when the Nepali tea garden workers became the worst sufferers. The closed tea garden workers numbering about 17,000 of Dooars (West Bengal) region is another glaring instance to prove the statement that they belong to marginalised communities of tea industry in a democratic country like India. This is because of the fact that both the workers of Darjeeling and Dooars are either Nepalis or Adivasis who are again in perfect sense marginalised communities while trade union leaders as well as managment personnel belong to the core communities of the country. This is another direct impact of globalisation process which has beautifully victimised, agonised and underscored the workers with flight from their two centurian living in the plantation universe. This is the award they got for shading their blood and sweats to the industry. Every time, workers are allured with false promises from every corner of the society, government, management and trade unions. In this way, they were under the process of organised exploitation ever since the inception of tea industry of the country. Now, they are under super-exploitation process, of course, in covert form. On the other hand, durnig the British period, they were under the overt exploitation process which was open and apparent for all concerned. Such overt exploitation was highly patronised by the then British government. After the independence of the country, every agency became passive spectators of the exploitation of the workers over which the workers had to live with innocence, illiteracy and devoid of any human excellence. Every one speaks with utter pettiness about their hardships but no one comes forward truely to solve their agonies in the truest sense of the term. This is the history of tea plantation workers since its inception to today. Thus, the irony of fact is that the Darjeeling tea industry—the national image of the countrty has nothing to do with socio-economic upliftment of the working class.

The Import Management: Challenge before Tea Industry

The post World Trade Organisation (WTO) era is Characterised by the blanket impossibility of ban on the import of tea from SAARC countries to India. In India, the Tea (Distribution and Export Control) Order, 2005 was hailed as a welcome measure to restrict the import of cheap or low quality tea whose production itself can not be allowed within the country. In 2005, total import came down to 16.7 million kilograms from 30.8 million kilograms in 2004. In 2006, India paid Rs. 119.8 crores to import tea against 97.97 crores in 2005. But import rose to 23.96 million kilograms in 2006. In fact, India imported tea from fifteen nations of the world. For Darjeeling tea industry, Nepal tea is becoming a big problem or challenge as in 2007, a total of 3.64 million kilograms of tea had been imported from Nepal paying Rs. 22.02 crores, Rs. 8.5 crores more than 2006. Thus, today, the import management and not the blanket ban on it is the greatest challenge to the Indian tea industry.

The Social Clause Paradigms

Tea being a labour intensive industry, 40.0% of investment to workers adds in the cost of production which is incured in wages/salaries. A broad guideline of the break up of cost of production is say Rs. 57/- (for CTC variety) per kilogram of made tea. This can be more clear if we see the table no. 25 of the study.

It is very clear from the table No. 25 of the study that 71.93% investment has to be done on labour i.e., on wages/ salaries/fringe benefits of the workers/employees of the plantations. The picture is more than one hundred rupees per kilogram in case of orthodox Darjeeling variety. But the industry can not end the expenses made on social clause of the workers. This clause comes under the purivew of convention (Dastur) ever introduced after the independence of the country. Some are purely oratory conventions while some others are there as per the provisions of Indian labour

Table 25. Cost of Preduction (per kg.) in Percentage of CTC Veriety

Sl. No.	*Item*	*Per Unit Cost*	*Percentage*
1.	Wages/Salaries	Rs. 21.00 per kg.	56.84%
2.	Inorganic/Organic Chemicals	Rs. 05.00 per kg.	08.77%
3.	Fringe Benefits (labour welfare, P.F.) Gratuity, Bonus etc.	Rs. 11.00 per kg.	19.30%
4.	Others/Stores	Rs. 20.00 per kg.	35.09%
	Total	Rs. 57/- per kg.	100.0%

Source: Bonnie Bose: Assam Tea Review: Dec 2007).

legislations. Thus, it is opioned by the management of the plantations that there is no second option left to the industry as a new strategy in order to face the challenges unleashed by globalization except to limit the manpower by increasing labour productivity. Of the total work force engaged in tea industry, 60-65% of labourers are engaged in harvesting season. They should be encouraged to increase their average plucking. The management also stated that 10.0% to 15.0% of price per kilogram of tea has been increased compared to 110.0% in wage increase within the span of last ten years. However, they stated that increasing productivity is possible through team work that is to be brought among the human resources of the industry. This may be the reason why Rs. 800/- crores have been earmarked by central government today in 11th plan period for human resource development and research and development of tea industry. This is one of the outcome of third Indian International Tea Convention held at Guwahati (Assam) on November, 22 to 24, 2007.

However, the social clause as outlined by the International Standards for the workers is mostly not strictly adhered to by the industry in general and tea industry in particular in India. This is apparent from the so-called fabricated tea crisis as beautifully articulated by the management and owners of the industry considering the tea price level that came to Rs. 97.79 per kilogram in 2007 in spite of the fall of production from 953 million kilograms in 2006 to 940 million kilograms in 2007, earning altogether Rs. 2130.73 crores for national exchequer. It shows that besides promoting the competition in the domestic market, the World Trade Organisation (WTO) agenda included maintenance of labour standards through the social clause paradigms. However, the Indian Government opposed for the inclusion of any form of international labour standard through social clause to the workers. Thus, the social clause is kept abeyance (Bhowmik: 2008), showing the sickness of tea industry. On the other hand, the minimum labour standards awarded since the inception of tea industry has been whimsically curtailed down today on one or other pretensions. In reality, if India is largest producer of tea, she has also the largest consumers than other tea producing countries like Sri Lanka, Kenya etc. which wholly have to depend on the foreign exports to sustain their industry. What is important is to produce quality tea at low cost to compete the recently imported tea from SAARC and other countries which have low price per kilogram of made tea in the market (Rs. 90/- per kg.) in 2007. It may be due to young tea bushes, low cost of production and committed management of tea industry of SAARC and other countries. The emerging trader-owners of the industry are overall responsible factor for such platitude of tea gardens of the region. Not a single new tea garden has so for been established in Darjeeling hills by the trader-owners in the globalized era as the profit so earned from the tea plantations of the region are invested in other sectors of Indian economy. The moment a tea garden fetches comparatively low prices or earn lowest profit, its trader-owner obviously left the plantation over night leaving thousands of workers in oblivion stating mere pretension as "Abandonment" of the garden for the time being rather than "Closure" considernig the consequences to be faced by them before the government. Over the last two decades, government too has nicely accredited such practice undertaken by the tea garden owners. Thus, hire and fire policy of government of India has been nicely operationalised by the owners to the tea garden workers of Darjeeling Himalaya along with other tea plantations of North Bengal.

Being an agro-based industry, there is no structural adjustment in regard to other factors of production in tea industry. In the name of structural adjustment venture under globalization, rather casualisation/contractualisation strategy has been adopted today as the recruitment method for the employment of workers. The Badli system has however sustained well to have at least one job to a child of the workers after the retirement of the workers. The question thus emerged today is whether tea industry is really the economic backbone of the plantation workers in Darjeeling hills or not. Whether it has sustained the socio-economic development of the workers or something else has sustained the same. Whether mobility of people from the plantations has contributing a lot to their development process? In fact, as we see that the globalization process has opened ample avenues for hard working Nepalis to shift their occupational loyalty to other services at Kolakata. Delhi, Mumbai, Chenai, Bangalore and other parts of the country and aborad for their economic development.

The apperent crisis in tea industry is also due to the mushrooming of small tea plantations in the country. About fiftty thousand small grower tea gardens have emerged during the last two decades. The mobility of the people brought change to taste for multiple occupations. In fact, such occupational options appeared before the workers families are due to the following factors in Darjeeling hills. These factors are :—

(1) The Gurkhaland agitation (1984-1988) and (2) Globalization policy of government after 1991. The liberalisation brought freedom for the workers from their traditional tea garden bondage due to the coloinal plantation

system which is still sustaining in tea industry, of course in different form. Unlike in the past, no manager or assistant manager of the plantation industry can call a worker by name or using derogatory words like 'Kanchas' and 'Kanchis'. Rather, now the management personnel have to call the workers with local cultural jesture, terminologies etc. as well as with etiquote of high quality like Daju-Bhai (brothers) and Didi-Bahini (sisters) whenever the management are to get the work done from the workers. Earlier, the managers used to call the workers with all sorts of rough treatment using the local derogatory words like Kancha, Kanchi, Chokra, Chokri, Lokra, Lokri, Marad, Aurat, Coolie etc. etc. The terms like Daju-Bhai and Didi-Bahini make every body delighted in the region that convey all sorts of respect and love. In fact, the terms Kancha and Kanchi if uttered by outsiders are understood in derogatory sense among the people in the region. Therefore, in order to harness the capacity of workers today, the management are trying to motivate the workers by way of organising some cultural and other training programmes. However, it is suggested that such ventures as the viable alternatives under the globalized social clause options may be adopted by all the management in the era of Liberalisation, Privatization and Globalization.

Kaman and Kamanees

Socially, till the recent past, the plantation workers were called "Kamanees" meaning thereby the backward people of the region. The plantations were known as "Kaman" meaning therby backward locations. The Kaman was to be called backward and people thereof were known as Kamanees as backward stock. By backwardness, two approaches had been clearly operationalised in the history of the Himalayan tea industry, viz., backwardness due to their isolation and secondly, backwardness due to the ignorance of the people of the plantations. The backwardness could well be sustained till the outbrust of Gurkhaland agitations in Darjeeling hill tea plantations when lakhs of people started coming down to Siliguri and they could be able to understand the niches for employment opportunities available at Siliguri and outisde. This along with the globalization of Indian economy ever since 1991, the workers through their family members staying outside, started getting well of the rapid changes taking place outside that have left ample options for their development. Every family of the plantations wants by now to have a small house at Siliguri—the gateway of not only North-East India but also Nepal, Bhutan, Sikkim and Bangladesh. Besides this, Siliguri connects the whole country in the truest sense of the term. Thousands of Napali students from Darjeeling hills opt Siliguri , Kolkata, Delhi, Chenai, Bengalore etc. for their higher studies and lucrative jobs. In this way, isolation syndrome (Kamanee characters) has been transformed durnig the last two decades. Prior to 1991, normally, the hill people used to scared of coming down to Siliguri due to malaria, communal tension etc. etc. But now Siliguri appears to be as good as Darjeeling hills considering the demography that reflects Nepali domination in socio-economic life of the people of Siliguri. Even the mainstream political process of Siliguri has to consider the Nepali community because Nepali community is the deciding factor to win elections especially by the ruling Left Front party alliance today. Another approach responsible for their backwardness was due to the innocence or ignorance of workers for present platitude that fostered well for the organised exploitation from all corners of the society till 1991 changed with their shifting occupational loyalty to other sectors of national economy. Now, their traditional loyalty to their masters in terms of ability to work as Khati Khanee Manchese/Jati has been transformed into the desire to work any whereelse in the country. This may be the reason why their children are exposed to global economy that offers multiple opportunitites (choices). This has enabled them to develop themselves in the cosmopolitan centres or cities of the country and abroad where the income security predominates the job secruity. Thus, the little known tea plantation workers of Darjeeling hills have been able to do away with their traditional bondage due to their ignorance to ouside world and thereby releasing themselves from so-called backwardness of the region. Further, they are fully able to do away with the curse of backwardness as they could be able to understand their capacity that encouraged them to adjust themselves to cash economy of the golden age of globalization.

The End of Labour Welfare

Ever since the enactment of Plantation Labour Act, 1951, the labour welfare of the plantation workers was understood to be non-compulsory in nature at the level of comliance by the tea plantation management. So, it was purely a voluntary legislation. This may be the apparent reason why management, trade unions and even government mechanisms became passive or covert partners of the organised exploitation process of the plantation workers. This was done due to the reason that the plantation was an agro-based industry. It means that it was as good as agrarian sector of the country. All the partners of the industry tried to establish supremacy over their respective professional area during the period of last sixty years of independence. That caused for the establishment of distruct culture between the management and workers at the unit level of the industry.

With the globalization of Indian industry, the tea industry has been reoriented from organised industrial sector to an organised agrarian sector. This has given birth to the curtailment of welfare measures for the workers under the so-called structural adjustment process in tea gardens. The issue like Gratuity, Provident Fund and Bonus have been the main areas of curtailment along with irregularity in wage payment, ration, firewood, housing repairs, medical facility, electricity, safety apparatus for hazardous jobs etc.

etc. with fabricated pretensions. Analysing the Gratuity payment of the workers, it is found that thousands of tea plantation workers who have retired from the plantation jobs on supernuation are not paid their gratuity during the last two decades or so. On the other hand, the government has also waived such past payments to be made to the workers by the management/owners. Interestingly, trade unions are also mostly found passive in this respect. Secondly, as per the provisions of Provident Fund Act, 1952, every month, 12.0% deduction is to be made from the wage payment bills of the workers and another 12.0% recovery is to be made from the industry and the total deducted amount is to be deposited to the Employees Provident Fund Organisation of the Government of India by the tea plantation management. But recently, it is found that only 10.0% of Provident Fund amount has been deducted from the workers payment bills and management also deposit only 10.0% as industry's share to the Employees Provident Fund Organisation of the government without informing the rank and file workers. Of course, it is also found that the management have taken the trade unions into their confidence with manifold illegal ways. Here, the workers are confused of the situation. Bewilderment of workers is found from every corner of the plantation system. For months together, the workers are not regularly getting their rations. The rate of ration is two kgs. wheat and one kg. rice per worker per week at subsidised rate as per the provision of Plantation Labour Act, 1951. Today, the Tea Board of India states that they provide compulsory rice and wheat quotas for the workers at the subsidized rate, and the Board has also started the introduction of the Targeted Public Distribution System in 2007 in the tea estates which has resulted into the reduced allocation of foodgrains. It indicates for the introduction of pro-rata system of ration distribution among the plantation workers which again indirectly benefit the management. Only the workers and two dependents will be provided ration at higher prices, i.e., the prevailing market price. This also shows the perceptible impact of globalization among the tea plantation workers (Assam Tea Review: March, Vol. 45, No. 1: 2008). The safety apparatus for hazardous jobs to be provided to the workers as per the provisions of Factory Act, 1948 both at the factory and field levels have also been stopped today to be given to the workers. To relieve the tea industry from the welfare burden, today 100 days jobs are provided under the National Rural Employment Guarantee Act, 2005 of the Government of India through tea plantation Gram Panchyats. But is is found that the so-called trade unions of tea plantations and their leaders as labour contractors of the schemes through Gram Panchayats provide the 100 days jobs to other than the genuine people of the plantations. This has rather created a huge stock of new proletarians in the plantations of the region. Whenever the workers ask about the welfare measures as they used to ask in the past from the management through trade unions, they make a lot of false assurances today to tea workers citing precarious financial condition of the industry. These along with other such reasons, workers mainly the male workers are leaving the tea plantation jobs to other outside jobs. Whatever the amount of firewood to the tune of two peals per worker per year given, it is just insufficient to meet the cooking problems of the workers. Thus, it is seen that prior to 1991, the labour welfare measures of the workers were of course inferior in quality while the globalized era witnessed rather complete absence of labour welfares. It is because of the fact that the very concept of labour welfare measure has become farse and far from bare reality considering the real plight of the plantation workers. It shows that the globalized era is not in favour of common human development of the plantations rather it may be very much favourable to a handful people only. May be the tea plantation owners are benefited from the globalization process in the industry but not the common people (workers) who are rather agonised much with hand to mouth problem. This may be the reason why workers feel that the tea gardens are the property of companies rather than theirs. Every morning brings all sorts of uncertainties to the workers leaving them in utter frustrations. This has also caused for their violent behaviours, depressions, deviation to work, suicides and passivity to the industry. The magnitude of their agonies is pretended to be unheard of or unnoticed by the management, trade unions and even government. This is completely apparent in gardens especially in abandoned and closed tea gardens of Dooars region of Jalpaiguri distrtict of West Bengal and also in Darjeeling district of the state. Lingering solutions to eradicate the socio-economic agonies of the workers from various corners except telling sad story with mere pettiness through various medias like newspapers, televisions, radio etc. appear to be the unanimous globalized philosophy to tea plantation economy of the country. This, in fact, proves that the tea garden workers are treated to be casual or unwanted citizens of the country as they come under the head of super-marginalised communities of the nation.

Coming to the question of medical aspect of the workers, majority of tea plantations do not have doctors and all the serious patients are referred to outside hospitals and nursing homes where the workers themselves have to pay all expenses. Although most of the tea plantations are provided the electricity supply by the government, the workers themselves have to pay the electricity bills. The house repairs and new recruitment of workers have been stopped for more than one decade. Very recently, the children education cess (at the rate of eight paise per kg. of made tea) has also been stopped. The roads are constructed by the Gram Panchayats of the plantations. This might have definitely reduced the cost of production of made tea but till today no management person has fully felt it necessary to be transparent about this aspect to the workers. Again, no management has stated that the cost of production has been decreased due to this, may be due to the fear that the workers may ask for just welfare facilities which have been stopped whimsically during the last one decade. This is another reason for emerging workers suspecion to the management of the plantations and also to the owners of the plantations. Thus, today, the tea plantation management have started to motivate workers to be proactive, positive and what not through different ways. Now, the pertinent question is whether the tea plantation workers will be satiated without getting the mere welfare measures from the industry as government has withdrawn to sanction any kind of labour standard under the globalization process in the country. All the welfare measures of the workers became redundent or less important to the government, management and trade unions of the country. Thus, the workers feel that they have been exploited in different fashions by different agencies in their own ways.

6

Socio-Economic Development of the Workers

In the present chapter, we shall disuss about the educational development training programmes for the upliftment of the workers because the globalization stresses for knowledge workers in the industry. To make knowledge workers, the Central Board for Workers Education under the Ministry of Labour and Employment, Government of India has also remodeled its training programmes for the workers. The Central Board for Workers Education established in 1958 to cater the educational and training needs of the workers through its fifty Regional Directorates and nine Sub-Regional Directorates across the country with five zones at Delhi, Mumbai, Chenai, Kolkata and Guwahati having its headquarters at Nagpur, witnessed an evolutionary mileage considering the educational needs of the workers during the various period of national economic development. Therefore, broadly, the origin and growth of Central Board for Workers Education can be divided into three stages, viz, Formative (1958 to 1981), Transitional phase (1981 to 1991) and Liberalisation, Privatisation and Globalization phase (1991 onwards). The Formative period is characterised by the implementation of trade union education in mainly organised sectors, the Transitional phase or period is characterised by the productivity education and LPG (present) phase is characterised by the quality and cost effectiveness education to the workers of both the organised and unorganised/rural sector workers in the light of declared objectives of the Government of India. Very recently, CBWE training objectives have also changed. The cardinal objectives as revised today are as follows :-

1. To strengthen among all sections of the working class, including rural workers, a sense of patriotism, national integrity, unity, amity, communal harmony, secularism and pride in being an Indian;
2. To equip all sections of workers, including rural and women workers for their intelligent participation in social and economic development of the nation in accordance with its declared objectives;
3. To develop among the workers a greater understanding of the problems of their social and economic environment, their responsibilities towards family members, and their rights and responsibilities as citizens, as workers in industry and as members and officials of their trade unions;
4. To develop capacity building of workers in all aspects to meet the challenges of the country from time to time;
5. To develop strong, united and more responsible trade unions and to strengthen democratic processes and traditions in the trade union movement through more enlighten members and better trained officials;
6. To empower the workers as employess of the organisation and to develop sense of belongingness and maintaining industrial peace;
7. To meet the needs of workers to have access to ways of acquiring and continuous upgradation of knowledge and skills that they require to find and held a job.

Considering the above mentioned objectives of the Board, the present section intends to highlight the impacts of workers education training programmes conducted in tea plantation industry of North Bengal of West Bengal. For the sake of analytical convenience, the North Bengal tea industry has been covered under the study. But before pondering into the tangible impacts of the Workers Education training programmes in tea industry of the region, let us see the nature and characteristics in detail of the tea industry whilch is the most organised sector among the other plantations of the country and their socio-economic development so as to observe the impacts of the training programmes among the workers.

Among the plantations, tea, cinchona, rubber and coffee are found in North East India. Of these four plantations, tea is the oldest plantation industry of the region. As mentioned in the previous chapters, the introduction of tea was associated with the denial of the Chinese tea companies from supplying tea to the British Government in 1831. One Major Robert Bruce discovered some indegeneous tea plants in Assam and thus tea Plantations were started in Assam in 1833 and the first eight tea chests were sent to London Auction Centre in 1838. So, in order to curtail the monopoly of Chinese tea trade in London, the then British Government under the Leadership of Lord William Bentick, Governor-General of India (1835) appointed an export committee to explore the potential areas for tea cultivation in India and the committee submitted a report showing the potential areas of the country. The areas as pointed out in the report were as follows:-

(a) The Lower Hills and Valleys of the Eastern Himalayas, (b) the Eastern Frontiers of the British Government with particular reference to the Assam frontiers and (c) the Nilgiris (South India). Off the above stated three regions of the country, the Eastern Frontiers (Assam frontiers) and West Bengal including the Darjeeling hills proved to be ecologically or otherwise suitable niches for the introduction as well as expansion of tea industry for British global tea market. Interestingly, the expansion of government owned tea plantations which were started in the beginning could not persist long due to the extravagent nature of British bureaucrats which was unsuitable to the industry and therefore private enterprises were adequately encouraged from 1859 onwards. In Tripura, the Maharaja Birendra Kishore Manikya started tea industry in 1916. Similarly, the tea industry was introduced in Darjeeling hills by Dr. Campbell, the Superintendent of Darjeeling at Allobari in 1840 while in Dooars areas of Jalpaiguri district of West Bengal, the tea industry was started after 1870 and the Terai belts of Darjeeling district started tea industry in 1864. Much after the introduction of tea industry in West Bengal and Assam, tea industry started at Arunachal Pradesh in 1987, Mizoram in 2000, Meghalaya in 1985, Nagaland in 2000, Manipur in 1999 and Sikkim in 1968. The eight sister states of North-East India except Assam and Tripura, are considered to be the non-traditional tea growing niches of the country. One of the major objectives to introduce the tea industry specially in Arunachal Pradesh, Nagaland, Mizoram, Manipur and Meghalaya was to terminate the prevalent Jhum cultivation or shifting cultivation of the indegenous tribes of these states. Secondly, the respective state government wants to industrialise the local tribes. Thirdly, the governments want to make the tribal entrepreneurship especially in hill areas of these states. Finally, the governments also want to earn some revenue from these areas of North Eastern states.

Let us come to the question of Cinchona plantation industry of North-East India. The introduction of Cinchona plantation industry was the concomitant outcome of Sepoy Mutiny (Sharma: 1994) when the malarial fever raptured the whole of Central India (Sharma:1997). So, in order to solve the problem, the British Government through Botanical Garden, Kolkata (Sibpur) decided to explore the potential areas for cinchona plantation cultivation in the Eastern Himalayas and South India so that the Cinchona plantation industry could be established in fulfladged form in the country. However, after the tireless efforts of British Government, a Cinchona plantation was started at Mungpoo area of Darjeeling district by Dr. Thomas Anderson in 1862. Considering its global importance, another Cinchona plantation was established at Munsong (Kalimpong) in 1900 A.D. in Darjeeling district. Subsequently in 1938, third Cinchona plantation was started at Latpancher (Kurseong) and finally in 1943, the fourth Cinchona plantation was established at Rongo (Kalimpong) of Darjeeling district of West Bengal. In 1870, another Cinchona plantation was started at Annamalai hills of Tamil Nadu. Till 1980, the quinine products had their main market in Amsterdam (Holland) and Spain. But after 1980 due to the introduction of synthetic drugs for the treatment of malaria disease across the globe, supply of Cinchona products has been completely replaced by other medicinal plants like Dioscorea, Epecac etc. in Darjeeling hills. One of the apparent reasons for continuining the Cinchona plantations in Darjeeling hills today is due to their ownership with the hands of the Government of West Bengal which has given due importance to the question of survival of six thousend workers of these plantations (Sharma : 1997).

Studying the Rubber Plantation, it is found that it was at first started in Sourth India during the early forties of 19th centruy. The Rubber plantation industry had been traditionally confined to a narrow belt of Kanyakumari district of Tamil Nadu in South and Dakshin Kannada and Kodagu districts of Karnataka in north. Later on, after 1947, Rubber plantations were started in Goa, Maharastra, Andhra Pradesh, Orissa and West Bengal due to their favourable ecology. These areas were called traditional Rubber growing zones of the country. After 1980, new Rubber growing areas were explored in North Eastern regions of the country by the Rubber Board of India on experimental basis. Rubber, The plantation project was undertaken in early 1960's in the then undivided Assam and Tripura under the forest and soil conservation department of Government of

Assam. Altogether, there are 44.72 thousand hectares of land under Rubber plantations with 64,628 tonnes of Rubber products in North-East India (Arunachal Pradesh, Assam, Tripura, Manipur, Meghalaya, Nagaland and Mizoram,). Most of the Rubber growers are called small growers of tribal origins without having their own processing or manufacturing factories (Rubber Board: 2007).

Another plantation product is coffee in North-East India. Coffee was introduced in North Eastern states during 1960s. The implementation of the scheme on expansion of subsidy to the growers by the Coffee Board started in North Eastern India in 1979-80. The Assam Plantation Crops Development Corporation took initiative to establish coffee as well as rubber plantations in North Cachar and Karbi Anglong districts. Presently, the North Eastern states have modest coverage of about 10.1 thousand hectares of land under coffee plantation. However, the coffee plantations are having some problems especially in regard to market network and higher cost of production.

Plantation Economy of North East India in Globalized Era

Altogether, 14000 tea plantations are functioning in the country today of which Assam has 850 plantations. Similarly, West Bengal has 356 tea plantations. Besides this, Tripura has 100 tea plantations and Arunachal Pradesh has 20 tea plantations. Still another eighteen tea plantations are found in Meghalaya, Manipur, Nagaland, Mizoram and Sikkim. Altogether, eleven lakhs workers are employed in tea industry in India. The North Eastern states produced 650 million kilograms of tea in 2005 with ten lakhs hectares of land under tea bushes. In 2007, 940 million kilograms of tea is produced in the country while in 2006, tea production was at 953 million kilograms.

After 1991, the non-traditional tea growing agrarian belts of Assam and West Bengal started to introduce small grower tea plantations without having manufacturing factories. About fifty thousand small plantations are found today in the country of which West Bengal has ten thousands, thirty thousands in Assam and still another ten thousands in South India (Karnataka, Tamil Nadu and Kerala). As estimated by the Consultative Committee of Plantation Associations, Kolkata (2007) fifty lakhs people are working in or associated with small grower tea plantations producing about ninety thousand kilograms of green tea leaves. In so far as the gross national production of tea is concerned, Assam contributes 52.0%, West Bengal contributes 25.0%, about 8.0%, from other northern states and 15.0%, from South India.

A total of twenty thousand hectares of land is under the Cinchona plantation industry in Darjeeling hills of West Bengal with 6,326 manual workers. Again, approximately 51,510 population of small growers have been engaged in Rubber plantation industry of North-East India.

About 180 countries of the world consume tea (Bhowmik: 2008). Till 1990, India was the main tea producer as well as exporter to the entire world. After the introduction of Liberalisation, Privatisation and Globalization policy in India and other Asian countries, the number of tea growing countries has been increased to 33 today while earlier till 1991, there were hardly five to seven countries producing tea in the world. Now, the Indian tea occupies fourth position after Indonesia, Sri Lanka and Kenya. However, after 1991, the tea plantation industry in India in general and North-East-India in particular has been passing through tough time in the global competitive market especially in regard to quality and cost effectiveness (Asopa :2004). These are found to be the cardinal challenges for Indian tea industry including North-East India. Yet off late, among the plantation products, tea is getting the global importance as tea has been considered as a health beverage across the world. Very recently, the import of tea from SAARC countries has become still another important threat or challenge to the Indian tea industry.

The Organisational Features of Tea Plantation Industry

Historically, the tea plantation industry was characterised by the immigration of Coolies (workers), heterogeneity of work force, low wages and coercion as well as indenture of work force (Bhowmik: 1996). Such characteristic features were completely sustained by enclave nature of plantations all over the world. The plantation industry was of alien origin (Greaves:1957). The International Labour Organisation (ILO) notes the term 'Plantation' at first as a group of settlers or the political units formed by it under the British colonialism especially in North America and West Indies. Prof. Hla Myint (1973) has distinguished the plantation system from agriculture by its large scale enterprises which normally requires more labour per unit of land, producing large scale products for business. Again, William Jones (1968) defines the plantation as an economic unit of land producing large number of unskilled labourers whose activities are closely supervised. The most important implication drawn from the above stated characteristics is that the plantation industry is the creation of colonial government all over the country. Secondly, due to the denial of local people from joining the plantations especially in West Bengal, Assam, Arunachal Pradesh etc. etc. due to low wages (six annas for male, five annas for females and four annas for chokra and chokri per day in 1947) eforced the planters/owners of the plantations to import manual workers from outside the respective regions or abroad. Except in Assam, Tripura, West Bengal, Sikkim and Arunachal Pradesh, the plantation industires are not in good shape. Among the non-traditional plantation zones (Arunachal Pradesh, Nagaland, Mizoram, Meghalaya, Manipur and Sikkim), only the Arunachal Pradesh and Sikkim are flourishing well as the plantations have not so far implemented the various provisions of labour legislations of Government of India. Thus, cost of production is very low in non-traditional tea growing states of North-East India.

Structure of Tea Plantation Workers

Among the plantation workers, only tea garden workers are conceptually considered as organised sector workers in Assam, West Bengal and Tripura being regulated by the respective state plantation labour rules ever framed in 1956. Rest of the plantation workers like Rubber, Coffee and even Cinchona today are as good as unorganised sector workers as they are not regualted by any labour act of the country. There are about eleven lakhs tea plantation workers in the country. Let us see the structure of tea plantation workers in the country.

Table 26. Tea Plantation Workers in India (2000)

Sl. No.	*State*	*Total Workers*	*Percentage*
1.	Assam	7,74,008	70.2%
2.	West Bengal	2,59,783	23.6%
3.	States other than Assam, and West Bengal of North-East Regions	43,463	3.9%
4.	Other Northern states. South India (Kerala, Tamil Nadu and Karnataka)	25,043	2.3%

Source: Sharma:2000.

The tea industry is a labour intensive industry. Quite a large number of work force is employed in it. The table No. 26 of the study indicates the fact that Assam tea plantation industry has accommodated highest percentage (70.3%) of workers followed by West Bengal (23.6%). It is because of the fact that tea industry is a traditional large scale industry in the remote, backward and isolated areas with agricultural work dominated jobs. Secondly, it is a family based industry meaning thereby that most of the members of a family are employed in the industry. Thirdly, work force of tea industry is consisting of various ethnic communities immigrated from various parts of the country and abroad. Fourthly, a new cross-cultural symbiosis has been evolved in the industry among the various ethnic communities. Fifthly, more than 54.0% of the tea plantation workers are females. Peripheral influence in plantations is very acute today due to wide spread influence of mass media like television, news papers, road communication, radio, mobile sets etc. This has resulted into the rise of expectation level of the plantation workers towards the plantation industry. The spread of missionary education in the plantation industry helps the youngsters to go out for education and training. But the children who go out to training and education hardly come back to the plantation industry. This has engineered the tea plantation management to exploit the illiterate or semi-literate work force calling them as "Coolies" while the managers feel themselves as Masters of the industry. Having isolated locations, the plantation workers join as manual workers and retire as an ordinary manual workers (Sharma : 2008) only. They are looked down upon by the wider society outside the plantations. The outside central societies called the plantation workers as Coolies. They have been provided some incentives as of an industrial society but the nature of of providing the facilities is rather a farse and simply eye wash to the government and general public at large. This may be the apparent reason why in some plantations, the percentage of absenteeism among the workers is increasing by leaps and bounds in especially harvesting season since the last one decade in West Bengal and Assam (Sharma and Das: 2005).

Plantations and Plantation Workers in North Bengal

The tea plantation zone of North Bengal has been broadly divided into three parts, viz, Darjeeling hills, Terai area of Darjeeling district and Dooars of Jalpaiguri district.

The number of tea plantation and workers has been shown in the table No. 10 of the study.

Table 27. Tea Plantations and Workers (2000)—North Bengal

Sl. No.	*Area*	*Total Plantations*	*Total Workers*
1.	Hill (Darjeeling)	72	43,259
2.	Tarai (Darjeeling)	46	30,800
3.	Dooars (Jalpaiguri District)	158	1,55,126

Source: Sharma: 2000.

As discussed in the previous chapters of the study, the plantations were historically characterised by immigrant workers (tribals from Chota Nagpur, Santal Parganas, Orissa, Chatisgarh etc.), isolation from the urban centres and low wages. Having such background, the plantation workers were employed as bonded labours in the plantations of the region upto the early seventeen of 19th century. The different tribes were kept in their respective tribal labour Dhuras (labour lines) under the strict vigilance of respective Sardars (labour recruiters and supervisors) and hence the inter-Dhura movement among the tribal workers was highly restricted (Sharma: 2003) by the managemet system. The exent of labour supression was so much so apparent that even the social relationship of the tribal workers was to be determined by the plantation management only. The issue like marriage ceremony of a worker household used to be determined by the garden manager. Having an isolated environment, the health and hygiene of the workers were very very deplorable. No one could express the grievances and hence they were treated as savage people to be tamed brutally and hence they were treated as good as wild animals of the plantation enclaves. Being pushed off the peasant environment of Santal Parganas, Chota Nagpur, Chattisgarh (Bhowmik: 1981) and Nepal Himalayas (Sharma: 2005) due to their acute poverty and landlessness, the workers had to agree with the colonial terms and conditions of employment in the plantations of the region. The same platitude was found with the plantation workers in Assam and other North Eastern states of the country.

Training and Education for Socio-Economic Upliftment of Workers

Considering the above platitude of tea plantation workers of the region (North Bengal), the Central Board for Workers Education through its Regional Directorate, Siliguri started functioning since 1975. The most important problem which was apparently observed among the workers was total illiteracy and lack of rank and file leaders among the plantation workers besides other indegeneous socio-economic problems. To promote the workers with the educational awareness for their socio-economic upliftment, different types of educational training courses have been organised ever since 1975 by CBWE, Siliguri chapter. This is evident from the table No. 28 of the study.

Table 28. Tea Plantation Workers covered under CBWE Training Programmes

Sl. No.	*Name of the Programme*	*Total Programmes conducted*	*Total Workers trained (1991 to 2000)*	*Percentage*
1.	Joint Educational Prog. (2/3 days duration)	377	9943	76.3%
2.	Self Generation of Fund Programmes (1/2/3 days duration)	36	720	5.5%
4.	Quality of life Prog. (2/5/4 days duration)	05	196	1.5%
5.	Leadership Development Training Programmes (one Month duration)	14	248	1.8%
6.	Functional Adult Literacy Class (Six months duration)	48	950 (till 1995 from 1991)	7.3%
7.	Special Saminar for labour Welfare and Development (2 days duration)	03	120	0.9%

Source: Office of Regional Directorate: CBWE: Siliguri: 2007.

The table No. 28 portrays the fact that the long term training programmes for the plantation workers for the duration of one month (Leadership Development Training Programme) or three months (Workers Teachers Training Courses) have been considerably decreasing ever since 1995 due to the non-compliance of the plantation level management who do not want to release the rank and file workers for such a long duration in training courses. Hardly, they release workers for once or twice in a year to undergo training programmes at the regional Directorate, Siliguri for 21 days duration. While they show keen interest to organise short term training courses at the plant level only of two or three days duration. However, the Personality Development Training Programme of 21 days duration of the Board appears to have been more perceptable to tea plantation management and therefore they send the workers for the training at least once or twice in prunning season (winter season) only. However, it is observed that the workers are found to activate themselves in such training courses as they are able to gather new knowledge about the socio-economic status of the workers around their plantations. This has helped them to develop their leadership qualities. For instance, the workers like Shri Mahesh Ram of Sukna T.E. (Terai area of Darjeeling district) who was trained in a Leadership Development Training Course has become the Organising Secretary of the Coordination Committee of Plantation Workers (North Bengal), Shri Alok Chakraborty trained in the same course later on in 1984 is elevated to the rank of District President of Indian National Trade Union Congress (Darjeeling) from the rank and file category, Shri Agapit Bara of Katalguri T.E. (Dooars area of Jalpaiguri District) is the Organising Secretary of Dooars Cha Bagan Mazdoor Union (CITU), Shri K.B. Gurung (Darjeeling) is the General Secretary of Himalayan Plantation Workers Union under Gurkha National Liberation Front, Shri Mahipal Subba of Mechpara T.E. (Dooars of Jalpaiguri district) is the President of Cha Bagan Shramik Sangh (Hind Mazdoor

Sangh) of Eastern Dooars who was also trained in a Worker Teachers Training Course at CBWE, Siliguri, Shri Shyam Kumar Pradhan of Ambotia T.E. (Kurseong of Darjeeling district) was also trained in a Leadership Development Training Course in 1986, has become a Sardar from the rank and file worker. He was awarded as the best Sardar in 2006 by local Darjeeling Gurkha Hill Council for his devotion to duty and able official of the trade union. As a good citizen, he has donated five Khatta land for constructing a school for the poor students of the workers. He has also constructed a Puccka road from the factory promises of Ambotio T.E. to the school premises. Talking about his quality of life at home, it is found that he has only one son who was taught at St. Joseph College, one of the prestigious colleges in Darjeeling. In brief, it can be said that the basic attitudes of the trained workers have been changed from negative to positive generating proactive approach in so far as their belongingness to the industry is concerned. They have also started to beleive on the rank and file leadership which is found to be the urgent need of the hour for the industry to meet the challenges addressed to tea industry in the era of globalization.

On the general parlence, it is also observed in tea industry that by and large, inspite of having one hundered and fifty years of the history of tea industry, the workers including the executives of trade unions seem to be inconsistent enough regarding the importance of trade union organisations and working class solidarity. It is simply because of the fact that the trade union leaders have been found tilted towards the management interests giving due pretension to prosper the Liberalisation, Privatisation and Globalization policy of government. This can be adequately supplemented by the fact regarding wage revision after six years in 2005 since its last revision in 1999 for the workers. The rate of revised wage structure has been decreased to Rs. 8 while in the last wage revision in 1999, it was at Rs. 10 for three years. It further decreased to Rs. 4/- today (2008) after agreement.

However, the plantation workers who were trained under CBWE, Siliguri chapter seems receptive enough to the fundamental meaning and concept as well as the diversified approaches articulated for trade unions today that is used to imply or entail in the manifestees of the unions. The socio-economic, political and environmental activities of the plantations, of course, were very steadily recognised and stressed meaningfully after 1991 by the working class unions. Here, it is really indispensable to admit the fact that in the past, the trade unions of tea plantations were all quite paradoxically lethargic as to the know - how of current trends emerging in regard to the progress of trade union movement in far and wide corners of the country. They were known as isolated unions as they were simply unknown entities confined at the inaccessible environs to carry on the orders percolate down to the garden level unions from higher central leadership living in urban areas of the regions. Secondly, heterogeneity of tea gardens in terms of multiple ethnic communities invited a fluidity of labour commitment from making their unions as honey bees which might perhaps highlight their approaches by comprehending a totality of woking class solidarity that could both in theory and practice be applauded. Thirdly, the lack of working class consciousness debarred the workers themselves to understand the real humanitarian base and entity of trade union organisations in the plantations. Fourthly, the population explosion might have been obstructing the workers for the formation and working of ideal trade union organisation in plantation industry.

Factors responsible for the formation of weak workers organisations were due to the ignorance of working class. As a result, the workers could not at all make themselves able to comprehend the humanitarian objectives of trade unions in the plantations of the regions. The colonial legacy owned management being infected by the British legacy of exploitation was also not actively taking care of educating the rank and file workers on trade unionism even upto the late sixties of 19th century as they used to think the workers as liabilities of the industry.

Inspite of having above mentioned difficulties in the regions, the late seventies of 19th century witnessed a favourable era for the plantation workers when the Central Board for Workers Education scheme was launched by Siliguri chapter of the Board. After that many overt changes have been noticed in the life of the workers through the educational training programmes such as Joint Educational Training Programmes, Need based Seminars, Quality of Life programmes for workers and their spouses etc. especially after 1995. In this venture, the trade unions are taking keen interest to sponsor candidates (workers) to attend the Personality Development Training Courses, Joint Educational Training Programmes etc. etc.

The traditional misconception of trade unions as the organisations of workers to merely protect and promote the economic interests alone is slowly but very steadily remodeled into the organisations which can rationally be loaded with multi-purpose approaches and orientations entailing the overall aspects of the working class which is the composite whole of socio-economic, political, cultural and environmental unit ever existed as an integrated entity in the regions that looks for national interest first.

The tea plantation workers who pick up the noble objectives through the training programmes of the Board have started recognising the value of multi-cultures that are surviving in the same plantation environment. In many tea plantations of North Bengal where the Workers Education scheme has been introduced, a kind of social cohesiveness has been evolved among the multi-ethnic groups considering the idea that the same earth is the common habitation for all concerned. For instance, a Nepali household invites other ethnic groups at the time of marriage ceremonies, Durga Puja, Tihar (Deepawali) festivals and other rituals. Similarly, other ethnic groups also invite the Nepali neighbours in several such festive occasions.

Very often, it is observed that the inter-ethnic relations are found to be very active among the workers belonging to various ethnic groups as they exchange jokes and gossipings at the plantation market (Hatias) that take place once in every week specially in Dooars (Jalpaiguri) and Terai (Darjeeling) tea gardens. Locally, the market is known as Hatia. Sharing the liquor culture (Hariya) might perhaps appears to be the common token of paying regards among the different ethnic communities of the plantations though it connotes unhygeienic practice among them in their day today life. Linguistically, every ethnic group knows the languages/dialects of other ethnic groups and communities and vice versa. Besides Bengali, the Shadri (mixed language of Santal, Munda, Kharia, Rajbanshi dialects) and Nepali are the common languages ever spoken by the plantation workers in Dooars and Terai tea estates while Nepali is the only language spoken by all the tea plantation workers in particular and Darjeeling hills in general.

But such things were not there till the early seventies of 19th century as all these ethnic groups were then the recent immigrants to the plantations and they were some how closely associated with their places of origin like Santal Parganas, Chotanagpur, Orissa, Nepal and Sikkim. That was facilitated by the absence of influential workers organisations with reliable trade union personalities. The excessive suppressions of the planters still carrying as the legacy borrowed from the British planters were still prevalent in the regions. Such pushback factors for reverting to their places of origin become very feeble with the passage of time as trade unions had started growing well in every tea plantation of North Bengal due to the intervention of the Government of West Bengal by implementing the provisions of the Plantation Labour Act, 1951. Moreover, the new generation of the plantation workers are so muh integrated and adapted to the tea garden life in socio-economic parlence that they hardly think of going back to their grandparents' places of origin. Such a desire for common living at the plantations as an integrated society has immensely brought about by the workers participation in educational activities like seminars, symposiums, speeches, trainings etc. that are quite frequently organised by CBWE, Siliguri chapter in the region. Thus, the recent approach that the trade unions are following is the departure from the traditional mono-oriented approach to merely protect and promote the economic interests of workers to an embodiment moving the workers from the micro tea plantation heartland to the national mainstream.

Now, the trade unions have started persuing the workers through the educational trainings as encouraged and assisted by CBWE, Siliguri chapter, to not merely on the necessity of cordial labour-management relation but also on the working class solidarity among the various ethnic groups at the plantations considering their distinct cultural heritages in toto and the challenges brought about by the Liberalisation, Privatisation and Globalization of Indian economy. However, it is also observed that the multiplicity of trade unions (now here are 33 trade unions operating in tea plantations of North Bengal) is to be diminished to a few in number so as to consider the working class as an integrated class by itself rather than a class as projected by Max Weber, the great Sociologist, in terms of market situation. Otherwise, in course of time to come, the very concept of working class would be rather a mishnomer or myth in truest sense of the term.

Quality Environment of Tea Plantation Workers

The major thrust of the following section is to highlight the findings related to the Quality Environment Project for tea plantation workers in North Bengal. The Quality Environment has two facets, viz, work environment and thereby leading to the quality environment of individuals and their family. The hypothesis generated is that if the quality of work environment of the workers improves than automatically the quality of life environment of individual workers will improve correspondingly.

Quality of work environment, as the name suggests, confines itself mainly to the internal issues of an organisation. This would mean the congenial working environment. It also indicates the congeniality among the resources in the organisation so as to bring best out of every individual functionary. Thus, the quality of work life includes the following:

1. The loyalty to the organisation
2. Commitment to the organisation
3. Participative culture of the organisation
4. Communication system of the organisation
5. Goal setting of the organisation
6. Properly stated attitudes of human resources of the organisation
7. Attributes of workmen towards the fulfilment of organisational objectives and development (Radhakrishnan: 1998). Kaith Davis (1976) has, however, defined it in a much broader way as "favourableness" or "unfavourableness" of job environment of the organisation. The favourableness of work environment in an organisation is taken to be reflected through :
    1. The system of team work
    2. Human Relation in the industry
    3. Productivity level of the organisation
    4. Job Satisfaction of human resources of the organisation

5. Safety systems of the organisation
6. Commitment and discipline of employees to the organisation.

Quality of Work Environment in Tea Industry

The history of human society is interconnected with the evolution of quality system. The meaning, implication and interpretation of quality evolution varivary from one industrial society to another depending upon its socio-economic setting. The plantation industry as a socio-economic system has also its distinct evolutionary history of quality culture. The quality of work environment in tea industry is not static. It underwent sea changes and showed marks of improvement with the organisational development. In this way, the development of tea industry since early 18th century, has been divided into three stages, viz. (*i*) Formative stage, (*ii*) Transitional stage and (*iii*) present stage. The Formative stage (upto 1947) was under the colonial rule. Migrant workers with low wages, family based jobs, coercion and isolation from mainstream of national life, identure etc. were the characteristic features of the stages (Bhowmik: 1981). The Transitional stage (1947 to 1991) was characterised by the advent and rapid growth of trade unions and labour legislations and the present stage (1991 onwards) is characterised by preponderance of employment of casual workers (Bhowmik: 1996), less government intervention or involvement in tea plantation affairs and industrial relation environment of the plantation industry.

The tea industry is a labour intensive industry. As mentioned elsewhere in the study, quite a large number of work force are employed in it. The table No. 29 of the study shall give us an idea in this respect.

Table 29. Tea Plantation Workers in 2007

Sl. No.	*State*	*Total Workers*	*Percentage*
1.	Assam	7,74,088	70.2%
2.	West Bengal	2,59,783	23.6%
3.	Total North India (excluding Assam, and West Bengal)	43,463	3.9%
4.	South India (Tamil Nadu, Kerala and Karnataka)	25,043	2,3%
	Total India	11,02,377	100.0%

Source: Tea Statistics: Tea Board of India: 2007.

The table No. 29 of the study indicates that Assam tea plantation industry has accommodated 7,74,088 or 70.2% of total working force followed by 2,59,783 or 23.6% by West Bengal. The South Indian tea industry has accommodated 25,043 or 2.3% of total working force of the country.

Quality Environment of Work in Formative Stage

In the analysis that follows, an attempt has been made to relate the quality of work environment with reference to some specific areas. This may give us some interesting observations in this respect (Sharma and Das:2005).

The niches or areas where the tea plantations were established were unhealthy forests and wage was very low. For instance in 1947, an adult plantation worker of Marad (male) category used to get Rs. 3/- per month (Bhowmik: 1981) whereas a village worker could earn seven rupees per month (Sharma : 2000). Further, there was no fixed hour of work. The workers had to start their work with the sunrise and to return their homes only after the sunset. Besides plucking, the same worker had to do hoeing, purning of tea bushes in winter, planting new plants etc. Such manual work for such a long period of time was regarded as unfavourable quality of work (Ibid) environment to the workers. But the management used to think such a job was easy or light ones. It suggests that the quality of work environment was the life of bonded servants and management personnel were considered themselves as the masters of industrial enclaves. So, the pattern of industrial relation between the management and workers in such work environment of tea industry was based on the relation of Master-Servant nexus. Least the workers could run away from such unfavourable quality of work environment, the masters as planters had obviously maintained their own paramilitary force. For instance, in North Bengal, it was known as North Bengal Para Mountain Force until 1947 when it was disbanded (Sharma: 2000; Bhowmik: 1981) for ever.

Each group of workers having distinct ethnic background was provided settlement in a labour line of tea plantation environment under the strict vigilance of plantation Sardars. Not that alone, the group had to work within their limited area without any interaction with another ethnic group. Unhygienic work environment in which the workers lived were full of epidemics, hookworms, dependence on stream (Jhora) water for drinking purpose, Kuccha houses of thatched roofs made by the workers themselves, absence of drainage system, latrines and urinals, transport and communication etc. These were the conditions of plantation environment. The workers had no voice nor any option left to them except to lead a life of bonded labours. Whatever the management thought better was to be accepted by the workers. Naturally, therefore, such commitment to work, job satisfaction, safety, productivity etc. that characterised the quality of work environment continued in tea industry (Sharma: 1997, 2005) till the eve of independence of the country.

Quality of Work Environment in Transitional Stage

With the independence of the country in 1947, the quality of work environment of the past characterised by coercion ended due to the change in the character of government policy towards labour because the government enacted labour law one after another during the period. Among the labour acts, the Plantation Labour Act, 1951 is most noteworthy to mentaion here. It sought to provide welfare to the labours and regulate the conditions of work environment in the plantation industries of the country. Later on, other acts like Gratuity Act, Minimum Wages, Act, Bonus Act etc. were also extended to the plantation industry to make the quality of work environment of the workers favourable. Further, these protective measures gave ample filips to the industrial relation scenario with industrial relation acts like Indian Trade Union Act, 1926, Industrial Employment Standing (Orders) Act, 1946 and Indian Industrial Disputes Act, 1947 in tea industry. The trade unions in tea industry began to excercise the right to collective bargaining. Number of tea plantation unions increased, various bipartite and tripartite committees were formed to change the quality of work environment in the industry. With the initiative of these agencies, the quality of work environment had been shaped to the tune of eight hours of work per day. Safety provisions in the light of Factories Act, 1948, wage revision at every three years in the light of West Bengal Plantation Labour Rules, 1956, and Assam Plantation Labour Rules, 1956, Puccka houses, health facilities, drinking water through wells and pipes, ration at the subsidised rate as per the provisions of Plantation Labour Act, 1951, children education cess upto the primary level etc. were provided to the plantation workers. But the areas related to increased productivity, commitment to task, favourable attitudes and discipline among them did not show corresponding improvement. On the other hand, it deteriorated so much so that strikes, lockouts and closures of the plantations began to surface during the stage.

Quality of Work Environment in the Present Stage

With the globalization of Indian economy ever since 1991 and thereby lesser involvement of government in the plantation matters, the incidence of strikes and lockouts came down to the negligible percentage compared the trend that was very much rampant in the transitional stage. It seemed that the industrial relation acts are no longer treated as the offensive mechanisms as in the past rather these acts are considered as defensive mechanisms to both the management and labours. With the emerging challenges as brought about by the LPG, the problem of survival of tea industry has become common issue for both the management and unions. This is one of the plausible reasons why unions and management do not want to linger strikes and lockouts today as were found in some tea plantations of West Bengal recently like Rungamuttee tea estate, Tirihana tea estate, Mundakote tea estate, Lingia tea estate etc. on ration issue and Bonus conflict in Assam tea plantations. Similar picture is also found in the plantations of other regions of the country. It is likely that such change is bound to have lasting influence and create a favourable quality of work environment at the plantation level in the present industrial scenario of the plantations in the country.

Some Pertinent Issues to Quality of Work Environment in Tea Industry

Broadly speaking, the categories of employees/workers in tea plantation industry are as follows :

1. Manager and Assistant Manager
2. Office Staff
3. Sub-Staff
4. Workers (plantation/factory).

The structural pattern of employment in tea industry is like a pyramid. Maximum number of persons occur is the category of workers in the field and factory. Secondly, it is a family oriented job as male, female and children of the family are employed. Thirdly, they are of migrated origins. Though unconnected with their places of origin, they have still maintain some of the original customs and traditions. Fourthly, majority of such work force (54.0%) are females as aginst 46.0% of male workers. Fifthly around 10.0% of male work force are engaged in factory and another 10.0% of male workers occur in the sub-staff category. Sixthly, there is very little scope for vertical occupational mobility from the workers to sub-staff category. The employment of 54.0% of female work force in the plantations has been associated with some historical background. Firstly, females are simple minded and sincere enough to their works than the male counterpart. Secondly, they render similar tender care and affection to the tea bushes and leaves as they do in case of their own children (Sharma: 1997). Thirdly, the fingertips of females are much more sensitive to pluck the qualitative tea leaves only. Fourthly, being assigned with double roles as housewives and plantation workers (Bhadra: 1997), there is every microscopic chance to involve themselves in trade union activities of the plantations. Females are best Hazira (permanent) workers who pluck 8 kg. green leaves and another 2/3 kg extra tea leaves daily. Now, the issue number one relates as to how to ensure a quality of work environment of plantation women workers in view of their numbers as also importance to the organisation and the family.

The perceptible change in attitude of both management and workers today in the plantations is due to the changed work environment of tea industry and also due to function of superimposed external factors or realizations from within—are the moot points to be explored to arrive at a concrete generalisation.

As it has been stated earlier, the plantation workers are of migrated origin and mostly they belong to the tribal communities having their specific ethnic cultural traits. The probability of change is likely to have been affected by the challenges to tea industry to survive safely in the competitive era. The second issue is as to how to make the plantation workers realize that organisational objectives and industrial work force objectives are supplementary to each other in the globalized era.

The expectation level of work force of the plantations have tremendously risen. The Panchayat system is also introduced in the plantation industry and the workers are now exposed to mass media like television, computer, E-mail, website, mobile sets etc. But the management legacy to ill-treat the plantation workers has not been correspondingly changed. A gap thus occurs, creating problems to the organisation (tea industry).

Now, the major issue before us in the study is as to how to bridge this gap between the plantation management and workers for ensuring congenialities in tea plantation environment? Let us share a brilliant experience from North East India in the following sections.

The Quality Environment Project

The Central Board for Workers Education adopted three tea plantations, viz, Rungamuttee tea estate under the Tata Teas, Tukdah tea estate under Darjeeling Plantation Industries Ltd. (now the Sycotta Tea Company) and Hilla Tea Estate under the Government of West Bengal for intensified tranining programmes of the Board. And in the process, a Quality Environment Project was introduced to address the different issues of tea industry of North Bengal (West Bengal) through the motivational training packages of the Board.

To materialise the objectives of the Board, a Quality Club was formed in the plantations in 1999. The member workers of the club were acquiring due respect with the initiation of the project from the fellow workers and people around the

Tukdah tea estate (Darjeeling). Later on, among the three tea plantations so adopted for the project, only Tukdah tea estate proved to be the most successful unit.

By the beginning of 2000, it was reported that the health consciousness of workers had gone up to the satisfactory level. Good health habits like nail cutting, washing hands with soap before and after taking food as well as after attending toilets, regular bath practices, cleaning trousers, keeping homes and surrounding clean etc. had become almost obligatory on the part of workers families. On the social front, there was a spectacular change amongst the workers as drunkards and druggists were not found roaming around the streets at night as they used to be seen in the past. More interestingly, it was reported by the management and local trade union leaders that notwithstanding the general grumbling, even the Thiccka (casual) workers did not endeavour coarse plucking that year (2000) at the insistence of quality club members. It indicates that the member workers had been successful in convincing the general workers of both regular and casual categories about the importance of quality tea for the sustenance of Darjeeling tea industry.

The second issue pertains to it was how to make the plantation workers realized that organisational objectives and individual work force objectives are supplementary to each other and it was being done by involving the members of the Quality club Coordination Forum (QCCF) and local political leaders in CBWE joint educational programmes. Here, members of QCCF meant the people who were associated with the social organisation like club, Samaj/Samities, Social Mancha etc. These people were related to both the workers and non-workers in some way or other. Moreover, the Darjeeling gardens of late, had been dominated much by the non-workers. In such situation, their opinion on the issue was obvious to influence the people on Thiccka (casual work) as it was a seasonal work to be done consciously because the Thiccka workers get the opportunity to earn something to repay their old debts. That was the appropriate time when people wanted to earn something more by not following the coarse plucking. Influencing such a work force from being not following the coarse plucking could really be considered to be the apparent success on the part of member workers to inculcate a sense of quality consciousness inside the workers mind. In other words, it was stated that the project was slowly gaining good momentum in making the people productive as a very important criterion for ogranisational development in the globalized era.

On the other hand, 2/5 days Quality of Life programmes of the Board were effective enough to bring about an attitudanal change in the minds of the people living in the surroundings of the plantation. The spill over effects of one such programme organised at Bhanjyang village near the plantation was found to have helped the people to be eco-friendly as they were after protecting the shed trees, tea bushes, shrubs, forests etc. of the plantation as necessary step for sustaining the agro-based tea industry as well as for the survival of the people at large. Thus, the fact that the organisational objectives punched with individual work force objectives was later on proved to be supplementary to each other.

The third issue as to how to bridge the gap between the plantation management and labours for ensuring congenial work atmosphere was no more a herculean task. The management who were attuned to realise that the investment on labour education was not drained in the coffen but a means to make the workers more productive. There was a time when the Workers Education programmes were considered to be the anti-management programmes. But after launching the Quality Environment Project in the plantation amids the challenges brought about by the

Liberalisation, Privatisation and Globalization for tea industry, the justification of joint educational training programmes of the Board at the plantation level became much prominent for the then felt urgency. The managers used to share the common issues with the workers at the joint educational training programmes and asking us for more and more such training programmes to be conducted in their gardens of the regions to bring about an attitudanal change amongst all concerned. Some of them (managers) had gone still further to organise Self Generation of Fund programmes for the Board to improve and ensure better work culture in the industry where they work and die for. It seemed that the people had started realising the fact that the development was not merely the increase of wealth but the application of human energies for sustainable development of the society along with the development of tea industry of the region.

Findings

Like developed societies, the tea plantation workers living in the isolated agro-based industry of the country were capable of adopting changes provided they were given proper training and education. The Central Board for Workers Education through its training programmes had sought to prove that quality of work environment of the workers was likely to be changed. That would require to put with the integrated efforts of the Board, management, trade unions, Samaj and surrounding enviornment for the mission. Thus, the unfavourable work environment of the industry of the past could proved to be favourable for the time being due to proper training along with planning being followed by actions.

The model of the structure of Quality Environment Project of Tukdah Tea Estate is appended below :-

Table 30. Quality Club Project Model: Tukdah Tea Estate (Darjeeling) Chapter

Items	*Broad Dimensions of the Quality Environment Project*
Objective:	1. To make the people of the plantation aware about the Quality Culture and Quality Environment. 2. To develop in them a sense of quality appreciation and thereby. 3. To improve the quality of life of individual workers of the plantation.
Hypothesis:	Improvement in quality of environment leads to the improvement of quality of end products that they produced.
Thrust Areas:	1. Personal Health and Hygiene 2. Family life 3. Economic Status 4. Education of the Children.
Structure:	QCF (Quality Coordination Forum) = 21 members (managers, trade union leaders, Samaj representatives) QC= (Quality Club) = 25 members trained preferably by the Central Board for Workers Education, Siliguri chapter, Facilitators (3 in each Samaj trained in the joint educational programmes-male and female).
Coverage:	At least one fourth of total population of the plantation could be covered in the first phase and would be given training by CBWE in joint educational training programmes for the facilitators so selected by the plantation management.
Functions:	QC members would be assigned with the task of implementing the project at the grass root level on the thrust areas with specific allotted areas and population. They would be assisted by the facilitators.
Documentation:	QCF Register with details of members and minutes of the monthly meetings,

QC Register with details of members and minutes of fortnightly meetings,

Register with details of persons attending Joint Educational programmes of the Board along with officers, guests etc.

Source: Office of Regional Directorate, CBWE: Siliguri: 2007.

Tukdah Tea Estate: Its Operational Phase

Phase I

Introductory (Campaign) Stage:- Campaigning of the objectives of the club, its significance in the present and other tea gardens of Darjeeling hills through the Joint Educational Programmes of the Board (2/3 days duration) during the next two years.

Phase II

Expansion Stage:– Introduction of Quality Club in other tea plantations of Darjeeling hills (2 years).

Phase III

Evaluation (Assessment) Phase:– Data processing, report writing, presentation of final report for further action or adoption of another project according to the changing needs of tea industry (one year).

After the training of the workers in subsequent three programmes in 2000 itself, the entire groups were divided into four sub-groups with four fold responsibilities related to the quality of work environment of the industry, viz.,

(*a*) Group A : A house to house campaign of awareness about the quality environment;

(*b*) Group B : Productivity Campaign

(*c*) Group C : Children Education and

(*d*) Group D : Health and Hygeiene. This would further clear the picture from the following table No. 31.

Table 31. Access of Quality Environment Project (Quality Club)

Sl. No.	*At Home level*	*At the Plantation level*
1.	Sanitation-Home latrine, urinals, cleanliness at the garden surroundings, drinking water etc.	Rearing and dearing of tea bushes and forests of the plantation.
2.	Health/Hygiene-Children education, health, occupational mobility: its impacts on health and hygience.	Care for proper handling of plucked tea leaves, stopping coarse plucking etc.
3.	Money Matters:- Family Purse, (family budget, saving and development of thrift habits).	Care for instruments of work and craze for utilising time and other resources.
4.	Social Evils:- Eradication of social evils (making old conception new).	Care for tea industry for next generation rather than self generation.
5.	Exposure to outside world by skill development trainings so as to stabilise the demographic situation of tea plantation industry.	Shift from old idea of productivity as management philosophy to productivity as the industrial philosophy-today's global slogan for all concerned.

Source: Office of Regional Directorate: CBWE: Siliguri: 2007.

The Quality Environment Project through the Quality Club at Tukdah Tea Estate, Darjeeling was an experimental project to test the hypothesis that if the quality environment of workers is increased or improved then automatically the quality of end products will also be improved. Functionally, it was in the formative phase as the quality campaign for better quality environment had not yet reached to each and every one thousand households there. It was expected to be covered by the end of 2002. A.D.

Quality Club and Neighbourhood

It was observed that to bring quality culture environment in tea industry, the neighbourhood should also be brought under the purview of quality culture movement. In this respect, the Board's training programme on quality of Life of Workers and their Spouses gives good impetus. A Quality of Life programme was held near the Tukdah tea estate of Darjeeling hills. As a result, it was reported by the management of the plantation that another Quality Club for the adjoining rural area was also being started very shortly in 2002 only.

7

Tea Garden Productivity Vis-a-Vis Globalization

The globalization opts for better productivity every day. The very blemishness that has been labelled against the Indian tea industry is due to the low level of tea garden productivity ever since 1991. The productivity of the agro-based industry like tea is the composite whole of every factor or very many factors involved in the industry as the tangible factors of production. Therefore, the present section shall highlight some of the pertinent questions about the factors responsible for productivity in tea plantation industry. The issue "productivity" has coined the day in the era of globalization under the competitive market economy. Thus, market appears to be very strong determining factor of production in the globalized era. Of course, this is directly affecting the working class of the country as a whole. It is more effective to the tea industry as it is basically a labour intensive industry of the country. Today, the issue "productivity" has been addressed merely to the workers. However, other factors of production also need to be properly addressed. But the major question is whether really the productivity of labour is a must today to compete the world market or not. Let us see the whole gamut of the story on tea garden productivity. The common perception in tea industry is that production can be increased only through the higher labour productivity. However, productivity can be inproved if other factors (material factors) of production are also improved. These factors include expansion of the area under tea cultivation, improvement in the age of tea bushes and replenshing of ageing tea bushes. Let us examine the situation (Bhowmik: 2008).

The total area under the tea cultivation in the country had been increased from 356,516 in 1971 to 434,297 hectares in 1997 which is an increase of 18.0%. If we take into the period between 1987 to 1997, the increase is merely at 4.6%. If we look at the tea producing states separately, we find a clear variation in the period (Sharma: 2008). The increase in area under tea in Assam, the largest tea producing state, between 1971 to 1997, it is only 21.0% which is higher than the increase at the national level. However, the more recent time span of 1987 to 1997 shows an increase of just 1.3%. In West Bengal, the increase in area under tea is similar in nature. The increase over the period between 1971 to 1997 is approximately 15.0% which is lower than Assam but during the decennial period between 1971 to 1997, the increase in slightly higher at 3.0%. Tamil Nadu increase during 1971 to 1997 is much higher than the two states and it shows more positive future prospect. The total increase during 1971 to 1997 is much higher in Tamil Nadu at 27.7%. This state presents a totally different picture when we compare with other states. During 1971 to 1997, it was merely 3.0% but after 1997 it increased to 24.0% in Tamil Nadu. The Kerala presents a negative picture in this regard. Thus, area under tea has been decreased considering the increasing percentage of consumers in the country. It has been understood that the internal customers has been increased especially after 2000 A.D. but the expansion of area under tea is stagnant. Earlier upto 2000. A.D., the expansion of area under tea was more than 4.0% both in Assam and West Bengal. The result is the continuous decrease in productivity due to old bushes and lack of expansion of area under tea cultivation. Let us see the whole picture today.

As it has already been mentioned that the age of tea bush is an important factor for its productivity. Normally, the tea bush achieved its prime notency in terms of output of green tea leaves from the age of five to thirty years. It can be seen that 38.0% of tea bushes are over fifty years of age which is considered as the uneconomic phase of tea bush and 58.0% of the tea bushes are over the age of 31 years. On the other hand, only 19.0% of tea bushes are below 10 years. This means that fewer tea bushes are being planted to replenish the older and less productive bushes.

The situation in Kerala is more depressing as 71.0% of tea bushes are over 50 years old in so far as the age of tea bushes is concerned. This coupled with negative growth in its areas under tea indicates that tea industry of the state is on the declining side. The West Bengal comes next in terms of age of tea bushes. Neraly 46.0% of tea bushes in this state are over fifty years of age. This is mainly due to large proportion of older tea bushes in Darjeeling tea producing areas although the Darjeeling tea is very famous for its quality around the world. About 77.0% of the tea bushes of Darjeeling are over 50 years of age leaving rest of the bushes sunder the tea over one hundreed years old.

We found the same situation in the state of Assam also where 31.0% of the tea growing area are covered with bushes that are over 50 years of age. At the same time, the percentage of younger tea bushes to the tune of 18.0% shows some bright future. Thus, from this perspective, the most prospective state is Tamil Nadu especially in Nilgiri district of the state as 27.0% of tea bushes are below five years of age (*Ibid*).

The foregone discussion clearly states that generally the tea bushes in the country are on the older side. So, much importance is to be given to replanting and replenishing the old bushes to incarease productivity. If this is not done then merely increasing labour procutivity can not suffice the purpose as the tea bushes do not yield the good optimum of green leaves.

Another dimension of bush productivity is the yield per hectare. It is also found that even if young tea bushes are there without proper maintenance (tea culture) then again the productivity can not be increased. Thus, proper care of tea bushes known as tea culture in planting parlance through irrigation, control of parasites such as pests, weeds, fungus, creepers etc. are to be done in time. These factors are equally important for even old bushes. India's performance in terms of yield per hectare is next to Kenya and Bangladesh. Sri Lanka is highest in this respect. Moreover, Kenya's growth rate is higher than India. In Indian context. yield per hectare is higher in South India than in North India. The two southern states like Tamil Nadu and Kerala have higher yield per hectare than West Bental and Assam. This is due to the better care system to tea bushes in the southern states than in northern tea estates. In case of West Bengal, the average yield per hectare is low because of Darjeeling orthodox tea. In 1997, the yield per hectare was 566 kilograms in hill tea plantations of West Bengal while it was 1864 kilograms per hectare in Doars (Jalpaiguri) and Terai areas of Darjeeling district respectively.

From the above discussion, it is clear that the production level in India has not improved comparing the increasing level of internal consumption in the country. For instance, in 2006, altogether 960 million kilograms tea produced in the country but in 2007, only 940 million killcgrams of tea was produced in the country. Thus, the production decreased considerably. According to Tea Board's estimate, internal consumption has been incresed to 15.0% till 1997 while today the internal consumption has been increased to 20 million kilograms annually. It shows that the demand in domestic market has increased while the price of tea has not correspondingly decreased due to foreign export. This may be the reason why the Government of India appealed good many tea houses like Brook Bond, Liption etc. which are the packet making companies to have reasonable price. Even the

National Consumer Cooperative Federation was also appealed to come forward in this respect (Bhowmik: 2008). It shows that in fact, the tea plantation workers have nothing to do in so far as price fixation is concerned. It is the retailers and people associated with tea auctions should give due attention in so far as the blending of tea is concerned.

The distracting factor for emerging above problem is due to the fact that during the present era of globalization, the internal consumption is on the increase while the production level has been stagnant. The question is—Is it the plantation workers solely responsible for this setback? The data state the issue productivity in regard to their negligence to duty has been decreasing not due to the callousness of workers but due to some other factors as deleneated below.

Firstly, the tea plantation workers have been experienced with the queer nature and low propensity of tea garden owners and management over the last few decades that they always hanker after prompt profits without replanting new tea bushes and also they do not want to wait for jestation period of tea. It proved that they are not really industrialists but traders. This conspires the workers to see for alternative jobs and engagements giving secondary importance to tea garden jobs. It was found in Bernesbeg Tea Estate and North Tukvar Tea Eastate of Darjeeling that most of the male youngsters as workers were found busy even in high plucking seasons carrying the alcohols from Jorethang town of Sikkim which is located at just opposite side of these tea plantations of Darjeeling hills. The hundreds of male workers are absent in the garden jobs for months together especially in harvesting seasons as they are found engaged in some other jobs outside the plantations.

Secondly, the work culture of tea plantations in Darjeeling hills has been disturbed due to political agitations in the region. Nobody bothers about the work which has resulted in the increase of absenteeism among the Hazira (permanent) workers even up to 50.0% in harvesting season.

This enforced the management to use Thiccka workers (casual workers). It is also found that the gardens are carried out with the Thiccka workers who in turn due to excessive greediness mostly do coarse pluckings. This has been found to have adversely affecting tea bushes in such a way that it has become very difficult for the management subsequently to make up the damage done to the tea bushes by such Thiccka (casual) workers.

Thirdly, the workers feel that the tea gradens are simply the place for constructing their own houses and grevyards due to the agenda of the Himalayan Plantation Workers Union. This may be the reason why today tea plantations of Darjeeling hills are treated simply as the abode of different problems and centres of political agitations for the sake of doing agitations only by the workers who are wholly fomented by the political parties and vested interest groups of the region.

Fourthly, tea garden management and owners want to earn money as much as possible within a short time without having long term vision for the upliftment of people and industry. A popular slogan is heard nowadays in the plantations is "SHORT CUT MAKES LIFE WEALTHY, HEALTHY AND WHAT NOT". The short cut in every aspect of tea garden life appears to be a new industrial philosophy mostly propounded by the management and later on followed by all concerned. It indicates that every body is in the same boat. This may be due to the uncertainty brought about by the globalization of tea plantation economy in the country.

Fifthly, in fact, productivity of tea industry is nobody's headache in Darjeeling today. The major political parties are busy with political gains from the region and hardly they have any constructive vision for the industry. In this respect, the Government of West Bengal has also very casual outlook as it appears from the approach of the government that

Darjeeling tea industry is peripheral in so far as the socio-economic development of the West Bengal state is concerned.

Sixthly, "WHO BELLS THE CAT" is the overall approach of government both at the level of local administration and the state administration in so far as the improvement of productivity that leads to quality of Darjeeling tea is concerned today in the period of globalization.

Finally, it can be said that the workers do not care much about the industry as they by now and then are able to understand the limited role of the industry for their socio-economic upliftment. The very difference between the development and upliftment is totally known to them having experience of the history of last one hundred and fifty years of the tea industry in the region. All the workers stated that nobody can really do any miracle in so far as their upliftment is concerned. Their commitments to the industry are not at all counted upon by the owners, management and government today as every company or management and government today comes and goes after accomplishing their selfish motives in the industry. Being the workers, they by heart and soul know the fact that they are born workers and will die as workers (Sharma: 2005) only. In fact, morally, the plantation workers are being dwindle completely during the last two decades of globalization. The other side of productivity like proper care of the plantation workers is almost ritualistic due to low labour standards. It is apparent from the nature of providing housing, rations, medical facilities, drinking water supply, electricity supply etc. etc. In fact, to raise productivity, the quality of life of workers must be improved or taken care of. The management always highlight negative sides of the workers and hardly they appreciate the workers for good jobs done by the workers giving some rewards. Even if management have been some how managing the plantations, there is absolutely negative solidarity between the workers and management in so far as their industrial relations matters are concerned. The negative solidarity may any time lead to total destruction of the industry itself. This may be the reason why generally the workers of a tea estates in Darjeeling said to a new Sahib (manager) as Naya Sahib Pani Afno Ullo Sida Garnu Ayo meaning thereby that this new manager has also joined the garden to merely fulfil his selfish interests in his own way. On the other hand, the trade union leaders of the region have also become very cynical on the one hand and utterly happy on the other whenever a new manager joins a garden as they will be able to exert pressure on the new manager for serving them better with good ransom articulated as per the dictates of situation along with intensity of the problems at hand. Here, the managers either utilize the local anti-social elements or otherwise follow some cultural jestures calling the workers as Daju-Bhai (brothers) Didi- Bahini (sisters) that reflect cultural softness and such cultural softness are appeared to be the easy way today as weapons to administer and exploit the workers comfortably. In this venture, the trade union leaders are also at par with the management of the plantations. These are the background factors why today the management somehow want to get the works done from the workers but they do not at all think about the innovation and creativity in order to raise the productivity of the plantations of the region in globalized era in truest sense of the term.

Politics of Tea Garden Management

All the managers of the plantations used to talk high about the Gurkha National Liberation Front (GNLF) under Shri Subash Ghisingh who had strong hold in Darjeeling hills till 2007. With the recent changes in Darjeeling hill politics under the Gurkha Janamukti Morcha (GJMM) with the leadership of Shri Bimal Gurung, almost all the managers are supporting the new political party of Darjeeling hills. This may be the reason why the GJMM has given relief to tea and Cinchona plantations off the strikes called during the recent months in 2008. Interestingly, tea garden workers of the region are not getting the wages whenever the strikes take place in the region including tea plantations. It clearly indicates that the political change is not in favour of the plantation workers because every political party and its trade union is in favour of capitalist owners of the globalized era. There is another logic today that present agitation is unlike the previous ones as it is being mainly guided by the town dwellers of Darjeeling hills. The dominant Himalayan Plantation Workers Union under GNLF has no locus standi today in the region. However, the tea plantation workers are being reorganised under the banner of Gurkha Jan Mukti Morcha of Darjeeling district. Interestingly, unlike in the past, Gurkha Jan Mukti Morcha has also made good dent in Siliguri sub-division of Darjeeling district.

Age Structure of the Plantation Workers

One of the parameters that determines the labour productivity is the age structure of the workers. The age structure of the Darjeeling tea garden workers is evident from the following table no. 32.

Table 32. Age Structure of the Workers

A (2000 A.D.)

Age Span of the Workers	*Male Workers*	*Percentage*	*Female Workers*	*Percentage*	*Total Workers of different ages*
20- 30 Years	6632	26.3 %	8800	31.8%	15432
3 1-40 Years	7711	30.6 %	6072	21.9%	13783
41-50 Years	8009	31.7%	10110	36.5 %	18119
51- 60 Years	1876	7.4 %	1980	7.1 %	3856
60 + Years	1000	4.0 %	723	2.7 %	1723
Total	25,228	48.0%	27,685	52.0 %	52,913

Source: Sharma: 2000.

B (2007 A.D.)

Age Span of the Workers	*Male Workers*	*Percentage*	*Female Workers*	*Percentage*	*Total Workers of different ages*
20-30 Years	4433	26.9 %	5380	17.6%	9,813
3 1-40 Years	3208	19.4%	14,720	48.1 %	17,928
41-50 Years	6331	38.4 %	3800	12.4 %	10,131
51- 60 Years	2080	12.6%	4387	14.3 %	6,467
60 Years+	442	2.7 %	2315	7.6 %	2,757
Total	16,494	35.0%	30,602	65.0 %	47,096

Source: Field Work: 2007 A.D.

From the point of productive age of the workers, it is transparent from the table No. 32. A and B that in 2000 A.D., altogether 11.4 % of the male work force of tea industry of Darjeeling hills were unproductive as they had already crossed their fifty years of age while only 9.8% of female workers were unproductive in the period. Interestingly, in 2007, it is observed from the table that 17.3% of male and 21.9% of female workers were unproductive work force of the industry. This may be one of the accurate reasons for decreasing labour productivity in Darjeeling tea industry during the recent period. Further, if we see the age composition between 41 to 50 years, 31.7% of male and 36.5% of female work force were most productive considering their age structure. It is because of the fact that the age between 41 to 50 years is most productive in view of their potentiality and experience in the plantation jobs. Interestingly, it is found in 2007 that the unproductive work force of the industry has been increased considerably. A total of 17.3% of male and 21.9% of female workers were found to be unproductive from the point of view of their age structure i.e., from 51 to 60 plus years in the industry. But the percentage of female workers in the age structure between 31 to 40 years had been increased compared the same age span with male workers having 19.4% only. The age structure in other various categories are more or less same between the male and female workers in 2007.On the average, the productive age of the female workers has been decreased on the one hand and male alienation from the industry of the region does not reflect bright future of the industry on the other. This is due to the increasing casualisation of female work force in the industry of Darjeeling Himalaya. Today, only 16,494 male workers are working in the industry while 30,602 female workers are engaged in the industry as regular working class of the industry. The percentage of the casualisation is almost hundred percent in harvesting season to that of permanent workers. Among the permanent male workers, twenty percent of them are either engaged as supervisory staffs or factory workers of the industry and as such only 28.0% of the plantation workers are males (Sharma:2000) today in the Himalayan tea industry.

Labour Productivity in the Period of Globalization

The labour productivity in terms of green tea leaves plucked was estimated to be 2340 kilograms per year per worker in 2000 A.D. in Darjeeling tea industry but in 2007 A.D., it came down to the level of 2280 kilograms per year per worker. Each male worker had plucked 1792 kilograms of green tea leaves in 2000 while each female worker had plucked 2340 kilograms of green tea leaves in the same year. Interestingly, it is found in 2007, a male worker, on the average, plucked only 1699 kilograms of green tea leaves while a female worker plucked 2500 kilograms. It shows that the male productivity has been decreased while the female productivity has been increased in recent years. This is another indicator for alienation of male workers towards the tea industry of the region.

Another reason for the decrease of productivity is alcoholism in tea industry. It is found that altogether 87.4% of workers are addicted to alcoholism of which 82.0%

belong to males and 5.4% belong to females in the industry. This has caused for many side effects to their physical structure including constant decrease in the body weight. Altogether, 67.4% of male and 21.1% of female workers are having under physical weight (Assam Tea News and Review: 2008). This may be one of explanatory variables for decreasing their productivity level. It is also observed that altogether 16.5% of workers are found to be indulged in smoking cigarettes and Bidi of which 12.3% are male and 4.2% are female workers. Again, 89.0% of male and 58.2% of female workers are found to be chewing tobacco regularly. This may be still another reason for decreasing productivity of labour in tea industry. Besides the above mentioned reasons for decreasing productivity in tea industry of the region, the age of manufacturing factories is another determining factor for the same. Today, there are 84 tea estates in Darjeeling district. Let us see the age structure of the manufacturing factories in hill tea with to gardens.

Table 33. Age Structure of Darjeeling Tea Factories

Age Span of the Factory	*Number Tea Garden*	*Percentage*
Above 50 Years	48	68.5 %
20 to 49 Years	10	14.3 %
Below 20 Years	12	17.2%
Total	70	100.0%

Source: Field Work: 2007.

Interestingly, it is observed from the table No. 33 of the study that more than 68.0% of tea garden factories is over fifty years of age, while 14.3% are between the age of 20 to 49 years and only 17.2% are below twenty years of age. Altogether, 88.8% of the tea garden factories are very old and it is found that most of these tea factories were established by the British planters. This appears to be the most important determining variable for emerging low productivity scenario in tea industry.

Optimum Utilization of Tea Bushes

Considering the optimum output of tea bushes, the round system on plucking of tea leaves is fixed in the industry of six days. Altogether, the tea bushes can provide green tea leaves for 36 times in a year so as to utilize the bushes at the highest level. It is found that in 2000 A.D, only for 33 times each tea bush was utilized for plucking green leaves. Unfortunately, in 2007, the plucking was done for 27 times only. It means that in 2000, the tea bushes were plucked to the tune of 83.3% while in 2007, the tea bushes were plucked for green leaves to the tune of 75.0% only i.e., 8.3% decrease in the productivity level in this respect. This is found to be another concrete reason for decreasing productivity in tea industry. It is connected with the recurrence of absenteeism problems in tea industry which is most peculiar among other industrial organizations of the country. An observation had been done on this problem of the industry at a very close quarter. Observing the problem, it is found that normally, there occurs 10-15% of workers absent and it increases with the payment of workers even up to 35.0%. Among the absentees, 10.0% are males while only 5.0% of them are females It is also observed that female workers normally remain absent on genuine grounds while male workers remain absent showing false excuses. On the whole, 90.0% of male absenteeism is on bogus ground while 98.0% of female absenteeism is on real ground. In fact, if we see the work load of workers, females work for more than 12 hours a day both in the industry and homes while male workers hardly work for ten hours a day both at the industry and homes. This is another reason for decreasing trend on productivity of the industry in the region.

Constant Management Change

A thorough pondering has been done in the study to know about the nature and time span of managers devoted to each tea garden of Darjeeling hills. This will be evident from the following table no. 34.

Table 34. Management Change in Tea Industry

Management Change	*Number of Tea Garden*	*Percentage*
Once in 5 Years	50	71.0%
Once in 10 Years	15	21.0%
Once in 15 Years	3	4.0
Once in 20 Years	1	1.0%
Above 20 Years	1	1.0%
Total	70	

Source: Field Work: 2007.

The above table shows that 71.0% of tea garden owners change their managers and assistant managers within five years, 21.0% of garden owners change the management within 10 years, 4.0% of owners change management within 15 years while one each percentage of owners change the management once in 20 years and above 20 years respectively. It shows that the changing pattern of tea garden owners and ownership in Darjeeling hills. It is because of the fact that with the change of companies, the entire management personnel who have acquired good experience in the plantations are changed. It may be the apparent background for the fluidity of the tea garden management in so far as their commitment to the industry is concerned. They are damn sure that they will have to leave the gardens any moment if their owners become annoyed with them. Normally, it is observed that a manager is given twenty four hours time to vacate the bungalow and hence he has to leave the plantation with bag, and baggages. Even in some such cases, the managers, out of disappointment, have had to leave the garden bungalows at night. This is the fate of tea garden management. The increasing percentage of management change is another responsible factor for low productivity in tea industry. It is because of the fact that a new manager needs at least three to four months time to know about the details of the new garden. This may be the reason why good many experienced managers of the industry are leaving Darjeeling tea industry to Nepal or other places or many of them have pursued their own business and tea consultancies in the country.

Survival of Tea Industry

The overall picture of tea industry today in the period of globalization of the region appears to be quite bleak as it is infected by the occurances of closure and abandonment. In the following section of the study, an attempt has been made to assess the reasons for this phenomenon along with the precautionary measures to be adopted by all concerned to save the industry from closure and abandonment. This is the lesson gathered from the closure and abandonment of tea gardens in the region during the period of globalization,

The abandoned/closed tea gradens are those properties that experienced many upheavals and changes in the ownership and sold after drawing benefits out of it. In spurt of debacle, the incoming owners utilised the assets to run the property by tacit support kept the dues mounting. The workers became impatient in a bid to recover their dues and their demands created a strong wave of hostility and protests. The growing pressure creased the critical rift and erupted in tsunami wave. It disrupted the normal work, uprooted the establishment and swallowed all solutions in its swept. The sinister blow caused multiple infections at various strata of injuries. In order to salvage whatever possible out of the property it was put up for sale. Having failed to get any prospective buyer the property was either abandoned or closed (for the time being).

Causes and Consequences of Closure and Abandonment

In course of reconciliation, the protracted negotiations failed to break the stalemate of differences. It was taught to digest the prevailing tension but the compelling situation made the workers subdued and learnt to live in acrimony as they were in the past accustomed to. The ordeal taught them to preserve patience, tamed them in facing practical difficulties and forced them to bear gruesome situation. The phenomena created a pattern of behaviour to absorb the environmental impact and restore flexibility. This form of adaptation is known as the somatic changes. The prolonged stress is expressed in increasing flexibility and decreasing reversibility. In the wake of perceptible diversity, it is compatible to mould them into the concept of survival incorporating realization, reformation, and adaptation. In order to ease out from sufferings it needs synchronization of system, integration of self-transformation and self-transcendence. The workers need restoration of self-confidence and self-organisation to come out of syndrome and utilize their latent potentials in framing their future.

Demographic Explosion in the Plantation System

The apparent dangers of population explosion are now recognised as it evaded all the preventive methods of voluntary phenomenon related to only fertility and contraception. In the wake of investigation, demographers confirmed that the population growth is affected also by powerful social factors. The lack of amusing pastime and recreation leaves a feeling of void and the emptiness which is failed up by passion of rushing carnal desire. The surge of sex acts as a stimulus for zooming lives in affluent sociaty, whereas it serves as a source of cheapest entertainment for poor people of the plantations. In pre-modern societies of the plantations, the birth rate of workers were high but so were death rates in the past. And thus, the population size was stable. The medical progress improved the tenure of life and developed better contraceptives for birth control but the controlled birth rate tempted to surpass the declining death rate.

Every species has the potential for undergoing and exponential population growth, but these tendencies are kept in check by various controls and interaction. When the system is distrubed, plants turn into weeds and some animals into pests and others useful species are exterminated. As such, the balance or the health of the whole system is threatened. Most of the tea plantations are having high population of workers putting more pressure on available resources and as such their qualities are on the decline. The surge of population diluted the human values and deprived them of sustainable opportunities to get job. It is in the interest of all to explore alternative arrangements to engage the surplus workers elsewhere retaining the required numbers for the tea plantations.

Need for Symbiotic Relationships in the Plantations

The symbiotic relationship is described where existence is recognised in a way that benefits all the participants. Accordingly, the relationship between employers and employees are forged of voluntary service and desirable sacrifice in uplifting the property at this juncture. The closed gardens are in dilapidated conditions, need huge investments and sufficient care in bringing back to active stage from static conditions.

The present hierarchy system of the plantations are more like tree than traditional system of pyramid. As a tree nourishment is drawn from both its roots and leaves. So, the power in a system tree flows in both directions with neither end dominating the other. In the interest of both the management and workers the responsibility and control should be balanced clearly. The investment has always been symbiotic relationship with benefits. The benefit of investors comes out from the plantation, manufacturing and selling of tea. The area from where the workers draw benefits are productivity linked wages, housing, water supply, ration, electric supply, health care, communication and cleanliness in labour lines.

It is an occasion to set the rights, responsibilities and control on a reformative way. Initially, it may look difficult but involvement of workers with determination can resolve their hesitation without depending on the management. The initiation of self-efficiency will drive out the feelings of complexion and a sense of competition would prevail. Once the workers compete with the circumstances they learn to generate strength out of their commonsense, initiatives and responsibilities. The workers on their own accord can contribute, manage and dominate on the essential services like house-repairing, ration distribution, water supply, electricity supply, communication and cleanliness in their labour lines and will have no truck with management.

The children of workers have access to good education in formation of their career and eligible to get jobs outside the plantations. The hurdles come in educating children due to paucity of money and the social barrier where the family members are addicted to bad habits. The family needs augumentation of income and control over bad habits. The positive impact of hard work gives higher productivity and in effect improves earning capacity. The short cut in income earned by fraudulent methods is inconsistent and rarely utilized in any good cause. They should be encouraged to open co-operative stores for marketing of useful items and entrepreneurship in solving the unemployment problems for able and disabled. These seem perceptible alternatives in symbiotic relationship.

Cardinal Components of Upliftment

The first and foremost parameter for upliftment of workers is their active participation. The initial participation is in the form of dialogue to acquaint with the problems of the property and ardent desire to resolve the issues without any reservation from any side. The revival needs the pronounced declaration of voluntary assessment of property, resolving the pending issues and current expectations by affordable means through negotiation and creating consensus in workers by clear understanding. The new agreement/understanding will start the work on clean slate without looking into past precedence, convention or commitments. They will have to understand the reality of the present picture and expect what is affordable currently. The prudent policy stands on developments to uplifting the ailing property without dragging back to involve in old disputes. In order to revive such properties a thorough restructuring is requring to change completely the old fractured system. It needs replacement by introduction of a new system as the repaired ones can not fit here properly and tends to wear out fast.

Involvement of expert Planters

The expert planters of long standing experience can be used to revive the closed and abandoned tea plantations of the region. It is because of the fact they have passed through all the ordeals of tea life and well versed in integrated tea plantation management. They kept themeselves absorbed in work and felt contented with whatever available before the advent of electronic media and faster communication. In normal routine, they created benefit/interest for the employer and displayed concern/sympathy for the workers. They can volunteer for the industry out of obligation that served them in good olden days. They possess clear conscious mind and can play a proactive role as a member of progressive civil society.

Need for the Innovative Entrepreneurs

The new entrepreneurs are exposed to global standard of governance and ethics. They understand the problems of small enterprises conveniently accessible to explore innovative solution in abandoned closed tea areas. Their adding commitments to socio-economic upliftment create a positive impact on focussed areas. If they want to utilize the ability to confront challenges and turn them into strength it is the right opportunity to pursure acquisition. They are not fact enough removed from their old lives to have forgotten the struggles the poor content with.

The State Responsibilities

The government should come forward to encourage the willing entrepreneurs with feasible schemes of relief to start the enterprise. They keep restrain in excercising undue pressure in passing through formalities of legal and bureaucratic barriers for clearances. Rather, they exert pressure in dislodging those involved in fraudulent utilization of public funds and disbursed for development. They must take adequate measures in eliminating corruption from soical life that is the dominant solvent in dissolving moral values and propagating poverty and treat the plantation workers under the purview of Panchayats.

Alternatives for Survival of Tea Industry

A clear assessment and understanding from the workers side is a Must in order to restore the tea industry in new form. The dynamic concept is foccused on realization of concerned workers who suffered the most in facing the stark realities. They had to confront the deplorable situation without any tangible support and thus have gathered bitter experiences on deceptive assurances. Their experiences have opened their eyes after recollecting the facts stored in their memories. Their wisdom is exploring a new direction for survival without further exploitation. Out of their own experiene of selling green leaves, they have learnt to realize the benefit of increasing productivity for higher earnings. By optimizing their efficiency, they are managing anyhow to survive in hardship. The hardship has remained to be reminded them the advantage of a stable management and durable flow of amenities. They repent in anguish and regret on the mendicant living. At this setting a perceptible quidance is required to ignite the value of a dedicated service in shaping their future. The inherent concept of dedicated service injects self-sacrifice that pays the dividends at the time when it is required most. The dedicated service has intimate relationship with productivity and there is cozy symbiosis between productivity and earnings.

The workers need to be encouraged to follow positive approach of contentment to accelerate the resolution of growth. Once the arrogance of envious attitude is subdued, the self satisfaction would prevail. It is not an easy task to make all understand in one stroke. If any new idea is inculcated then some gets faster understanding, some takes time to percolate it down but some die-hards are deterred to accept it at all. The understanding lies in the heads and rest all are symptoms. The heterogeneous society constitutes of all types of people and needs variable motivations for reformation. The inclination towards voluntary involvement in accepting responsibilities will initiate silent transformation in disssolving the long standing bitterness.

The basic concept lies in the participation of workers in the management of property with their intuitive understanding of life and death. They are tired of suffering in anguish and wandering through ideological therapy in search of survival. Finding no relief through various ideological therapies, they have lost faith in them. They felt neglected and questioned about their respect and identity. The situation has taught them tolerance and brought enduring prudence in adversity. The volunteerism is the only guarantee to restore their self-respect and recover the lost identity. They need to take willingly the most fundamental self-reflection on the condition of property and its limited ability to facilitate their needs at this juncture. The first priority is given for physical survival and the second part is for its maintenance and the rests are considered secondary in crisis. Their fading memory still reminds them of old primitive activities in persuasion to get more that did not bring them transient promises, devoid of durable peace and destructive attitudes through abusive exploitations. If they understand reformation rationally and intend to start a fresh chapter in life then learn to take lesson from the past mistakes. The complimentary tendencey of healing and adaptation contribute to become constructive and creative. In order to save them from toying in delusions, the reactive mind is provided to secure survival. The sanity is restored by the release of the suggestion into consciousness.

Therefore, workers must develop courage in facing outcome of reality not the expectation of mirage illusion. They ought to understand that ruthlessly damaged properties are inflicted with deep wounds, need proper dressing and take its own time in recovery. The abandoned tea plantations can not be compared with well off gardens where resources are avilable and infrastructures intact. It needs investment of money, time and energy in a pragmatic provision to rebuild the system. The broken infrastructure of abandoned tea plantations can not be restored in haste and the development work takes its own gestation period to give productive results. Similary, the restoration of amenities it based on desirable recovery and gaining strength in order to bear more burdens. The process of recovery is a time consuming period and needs enough patience of dissension to understand it. The mere display to any deliberate excitment is liable to jeopardize the flow of progress and delay the recovery, the reformation is a slow process and its alliances are the components of forbearance and endeavour. The salient feature in the struggle for existence defines confronting challenges against the current of adverse conditions. The concept conceives the idea of self-assured determination to accept challenges in the midst of disssension and diversity. The philosophy encompasses to one and all involved in the process of transformation with out any touch of pride and prejudice.

Contributions and assistance of experienced planters is another way for restoring the lost glory of tea industry of the region. The concept of management in radical reformation casts an apparent impact on the emergence of simple and transparent system of control. The management is required to come out from clusters of old colonial culture and foster a multi-culture environment. They need to follow proactive suggestions and deal with workers in sporting manner. The restructured nomenclature from manager to tea farmer reflects a down to earth type person having a fair knowledge of tea plantation problems and its rational solutions. The supervisory staffs need to be selected out of existing workers and promoted after proper training. The tea farmer and trained persons are responsible in imparting training to workers on the guide lines of adopted philosophy. The integrity in dealing, easily approachable and simple-living are considered the basic code of conduct. In order to remain debt free, all are advised to live within means avoiding transactions on credit. The tea farmer will have to earn his living by displaying his initiative, action and achievement in finding a rational way of survival. Everyone involved in the process of silent revolution will have to show solidarity in support of mission.

The overall administration is supervised by a consortium of experienced tea planters who belong to progressive civil society and concerned with problems of abandoned/closed tea platations. They have concerned with problems that they have passed through in life and familiar in mixing arrogance and humility to form a harmonic cocktail. Their proactive role demands to invite them for their support in the form of obligation to tea industry that sustained them and their families as in good olden days. They should avail the opportunities to visit the ailing properties, analyze the findings, make a comprehensive report and submit in a form suitable for ailing gardens. The local body of management will be fully involved in discussion and mode of implementation. The decision is implied on implicit assessment and self-introspection. There is no place of blame and counter blame in the system but it is imporant to point out the mistakes at the earliest to make a quick rectification.

The Commitments and Invovation of Entrepreneurs

The prospective investors must take as a challenging enterprise for fast development and speedy recovery of ailing tea plantations. Initial investement is very high in case of closed/abandoned gardens but a pragmatic approach can always be explored graden-wise into its viable aspects. The fair play in management and transparencey in accounting system keeps the management above board. The trust in management entails co-operation in solving many complicated problems and create confidence in correct evaluation of performance.

It is very essential to understand the finer tuning in achievement of production, productivity and quality. The entire result is connected with productive and developmental systems. The high productivity is related to efficient plucking by pluckers, existene of good tea stand, free from pests and diseases along with favourable weather.

It is not out of place to mention here that agriculture based tea is directly influenced by the vegaries of weather. The frequent change in erratic-behaviour of weather is due to ecological distrubances and affects the crop prospects in varying degree. The extreme climate of incessant rain charges rivers in furious flow breaking its banks to invade tea plantations. The roads are washed out, bridges are broken, electric lines is snapped and grid power suspended. The inclement weather does intense damage to labour lines and uproot standing shade trees damaging tea bushes along with it. The razing hail-storms strip the plantation even by debanking and damaging rest of the property. The blistering heat bakes the planted areas farming cracked floor and growth ceased.

The ecological changes and scathing pesticides have contributed evolutionary cause in breeding of hardy pests and diseases. They invade tea plantation menancingly and evade all the teachique of control even by latest generation of pesticides. In absence of control they leave the area stripped. It takes ample time in recovery to get crop from the area. When the healty gardens feel the harsh brunt of weather and severe attack of pests and diseases, the sick gardens face terminal sickness of intensive care.

Need for Change in Cultural Practices on Tea Gardens

It is ecologically sustainable farming that contains huge potential with high demand. The soils of closed/abandoned gradens are hungry without proper fertilization and the bushes are dilapidated by pests and diseases. The concept of organic fertilization in based upon the principle or replanishment of whatever is taken out from soil. The organic fertilizer is composed of organic materials, inorganic materials in its natural form, vermi and vegetaion composts and bio-fertilizers. The organic farming shows its result slowly but firmly without any contra effect. It preserves the nutrients of soils and protects from degradation. Where there is synergy and cultural fit it makes the best use of resources. It improves the quality of the end product, maintains ecological balance and protects workers from health hazards. Organic tea commands better values in the international market.

Relief System of the Government

The aspiring entrepreneurs want a very clear picture of assistance available from the government before plunging in challenging venture. The government with feasible schemes needs to come forward showing clearly the road map of revival considering the interests of investors. They spell clearly who will pay the old liabilities accumulated through many years as the new entrepreneurs are only interested in safe investments. The investors are least interested in increasing the burden. And all or interested to know the current burdens of statutory provisions can be selectively phased out/deferred. The relief so far offered is a half- hearted process and not a tangible form to attract new entrepreneurs.

As a welfare state based on the socialistic pattern of society, the governments are responsible to take adequate mesures in the development of socio-economic status and health care of all. They should extend their infrastructure to stimulate multi-skilled programmes for self-employment and helping in welfare scheme as foundation of progress. As plantations come under "Panchayat" all plantation residents are equally entitled to avail all the facilities as available to villagers and busty-dwellers.

It is a well known fact that both the state and central governments have their own agenda under political manifesto to dominate over voters and display interests in their welfare. The random favour was extended without going into latent details of garden problems, served meagre satisfation of unsustainable nature. Their agency needs to delve deeper in diagnosing the deep rooted ailments of gardens and then prescribe the effective measures in bringing relief. More gardens are grasping for tangible support in maintaining the existential half. The new entrepreneurs are hesitant to join the complicated system characterised by intemperate thurst for power and plagued by social and ideological conflicts. The governments need to focus on prevention of corruption that is the dominant solvent in dissolving moral values and creating poverty (Verma: 2008).

Human Resource Development Scheme

In order to improve the socio-economic life of tea plantation workers so as to address the forces of globalization, very recently, the Government of India has sanctioned Rs. 50/_ crores of which Rs. 31.60 crores are to be utilised for drinking water, sanitation, educational stipend for the children of workers, extension and construction of schools in tea gradens, medical facilities, construction of garden hospitals, assistance to the disabled persons dependent on tea garden workers, sports etc. Remaining Rs. 18.40 crores is to be utilised for training programmes. These schemes are mainly meant for hill tea plantations of North East India (Tea Board of India: 2007). The scheme has no entry into the tea plantations of Darjeeling hills and other tea plantations of West Bengal. Thus, the social gains due to the sanction of Rs. 50 crores is hundreed percent absent to the tea plantations of Darjeeling hills till today.

Panchayati Raj Schemes in Tea Plantations

It is found that almost all the tea plantations of the region have rejected the schemes apparently apprehending that schemes will create lot of problems to the industry. For instance, Indira Avas Yogana, Pradhan Mantri Sadak Yogana etc. etc. Take for instance of Indira Avas Yogana to which the owners of tea gardens feel that once the workers are covered under the scheme, they will loose their ownership right of the workers Dhuras (labour lines) which they feel is their colonies even today as in the British time. Similarly, take the case of Pradhan Mantri Sadak Yogana. Here is this aspect too, the owners apprehends that if a road is constructed, then there will be a free flow of people of wider society and make their workers liberalised in all aspects of their life. Thus, they can not manage the workers as per their dictates. Again, regarding Swarnajayanti Gram Rozgar Yogana under the Panchayti Raj institutions, in relation to tea plantations, it is found that some people who in fact not realy genuine workers are enjoying the benefits completely. Coming to the question of Rural Water Supply Scheme, Rural Sanitation Scheme, Hariyali Scheme etc. etc. In tea plantations of the region mostly they are only in paper. These schemes are simply found to be cracked down being swallowed by the vested interest people. The owners have rather whimsically assured the government that they will do these jobs by themselves. It is due to the problem of proper governance and devotion of government or improper devolution of power to the inappropriate people of the region. The tea garden management are always concerned with profit than socio-economic upliftment of tea garden workers. It is in fact that the Panchayati Raj system is a far cry in tea plantation industry of the region.

Tea Tourism of the Government

The basic objective behind the sanction of rupees twenty crores for tea tourism project by the Government of West Bengal in 2007 is not meant for Darjeeling hill tea plantations because the issue tourism comes under the purview of Darjeeling Gurkha Hill Council. The DGHC since its formation (1988) has played very negligible role on this aspect because DGHC is found to have busy with merely constructing community centres without developing the basic infrastructure like road, water supply, electricity, education etc. etc. for the tea plantation workers. In fact, the tea garden workers comes under the purview of state list of the Indian Constitution and basically the plantation workers are agricultural workers. So, the socio-economic development of tea plantations through tea tourism is a political gimmick of the Government of West Bengal specially in so far as the Darjeeling hills is concrened.

Labour Productivity in the Himalayan Tea Industry: Concluding Remark

In fact, measurement of labour productivity in the Himalayan tea industry is quite difficult task due to its dominant agrarian nature. Thus, in reality, labour productivity in tea industry is really difficult due to the following factors:

(*i*) It is difficult to count the exact number of productive workers because of the absence of authentic data, (*ii*) it is difficult to evaluate performances of various skills and intensity involved at different stages of production, (*iii*) it is due to seasonal character of workers requirements (Lama:1986).The basic tenets for increasing productivity is absent in Darjeeling tea industry. It is because of the fact that the very concept of productivity is not really comprehended holistically by all concerned. Productivity is the state of human mind which can only harness all the factors of production including human capital. The biased outlook from different corners like management, owners and government to labour can not reap meaningful increase in productivity. In fact, till today, the management personnel have not been able to make the productivity as an industrial philosophy rather than the management philosophy. This is the reason why workers think that the issue 'productivity' is management subject and they have nothing to take it so seriously to materialize into their work culture. Still another reason for this is that the workers did not get proper fruits of productivity in terms of their socio-economic development. The garden productivity, so far, did not create symbiotic relationship between the workers and management. This makes the workers totally unsatisfied and disgruntled and quite often, they shift their loyalty to not only outside jobs but also involving themselves in new political agitations. The statement can be supplemented by their changing political loyalty from Gurkha National Liberation Front to Gurkha Ganamukti Morcha party today. The GNLF did nothing for the cause of the Himalayan plantation workers during the last two decades. This may be the reason why today hundred percent of tea and cinchona plantation workers of Darjeeling Himalaya is in favour of Gurkha Ganamukti Morcha. They do so as they said that Bhir Bara Laree Pani Kilo Ritai, Bag Le Khai Pani Kilo Ritai meaning thereby whether their cow is fell from the hill tops or eaten by tiger is same for them. Whether this company or that company as well as this management or that management comes or goes, their agonies are same for ever. It means that the history of one hundred and fifty years of tea industry did not make the working class excellence with organizational development and individual class development as complimentary to each other. The mollified intentions of tea garden owners as traders and management as the hawkers of owners (traders) are responsible for such platitude of tea industry in the region. The traders (owners)-Management (hawkers) Raj (Sharma and Das: 2008) on the one hand and Management-Contractors (local trade union leaders) Raj on the other as well as Hawkers/Contractors-Gajir (government servants associated with tea industry) Raj are prevailing philosophy of tea industry in the region. The commission culture is still another strong thread for manipulation everything in the plantation industry and it makes the semi-literate or illiterate tea plantation workers super-exploited. Whatever the decisions are taken on tea plantation industry and workers, they are taken either at Kolkata or Siliguri. So, no rank and file worker knows anything about the contents and circumstances of decision making and agreements done among the partners of the industry. This is evident from the observation made from the opinions of the workers. Now, every tea and cinchona plantation worker of the region said that Shri N.K. Kumai, the President of the Himalayan Plantation Workers earned crores of rupees as a great hawker of tea garden management during the last two decades and now enjoying his retired life at Darjeeling or Siliguri or Kolkata. So, to raise productivity as a state of mind, who will do this since the very work culture of the plantations has been totally deteriorated by Management—Trade Union—Nasty Nexus.

So, to raise productivity, work culture is to be improved first from the top management and trade union executives and it can be adequately percolated down to the rank and file tea plantation workers. The mollified approach and false pretensions of management and trade union leaders/executives can no more convince the workers for better work culture and thereby the increase of productivity. It is therefore a herculean task before them in the era of globalization and it has posed great threat to the industry in the global tea trading competition There is nothing in fact the problem of labour productivity but lack of vision, mission and creativity among the owners-management-trade union as well as government agencies in the light of globalization. Simply following the British legacy by the management can reap no fruit especially on issue like productivity. The capacity of human resource is unlimited but how it can be properly harnessed is a human issue that involves care and satisfaction of the workers by the industry. Hands can be forced to work but not the head and heart of the workers. So, to capture the head and heart is not an easy business. It requires genuine services to be rendered to the working class. So, to win the confidence from head and heart of the workers is only option left to the management for raising productivity in the Himalayan tea industry.

8

Health Dimensions of the Workers : Tradition Vs. Modernity

The synchronized Hindu-Budhist traditions of the Himalayan regions (Sharma: 2003) had since time immemorial institutionalized the mixed blend of healing practices among the indegeneous tribes and sub-tribes of Nepal and North Eastern Himalayas. The major thrust of present section of the study is to highlight ordelineate the nature and type of *Dhami-Jhakris* (Shahmen)—the traditional health healers and their roles among the tea plantation workers of Darjeeling hills of Eastern Himalaya. Conceptually, the entire population belonging to the plantation workers of Darjeeling hills has been divided into Tagadhari and Matwali groups of the Nepali society (Sharma: 2003). Broadly speaking, the Nepali society is consisting of Aryan (Tagadharis) and Mongoloid (Matwalis) stocks. Except the Bahun, Chhetri and Thakuri, all other castes like Rai, Limboo, Tamang, Newar, Sunuwar, Thami, Gurung, Mangar, Sherpa, Bhutia, Lepcha etc. mainly belong to Mongoloid (Matwalis) stock. This may be the reason why one after another, these Matwali castes have been converted into scheduled tribes and other backward class (OBC) categories in the region. This can be supplemented by the fact that very recently the Tamang and Limboo castes of the Nepali society have been converted into Scheduled tribes in Darjeeling-Sikkim Himalayas. Further, it is also supported by the fact that Shri Subash Ghising, the Chairman of Darjeeling Gurkha Hill Council, had been demanding for the inclusion of Darjeeling hills as tribal area under the sixth schedule of Indian Constitution. The same thing is also found in case of Sikkim where Tamang and Limboo castes have already got tribal status and all other Nepali castes have been given the status of Other Backward Classes in Sikkim. In the past, the Matwalis who were mostly tribes and sub-tribes of Nepal and the Eastern Himalayas including the North East India along with the Tagadharis used to employ respective caste and tribal Dhami-Jhakris to cure their patients. Today, the Dhami-Jhakris are still found to be quite popular in Kaman-Bustees (plantations-villages) of Darjeeling and Sikkim including North-East India.

The establishment of Labour Dhuras (lines) in tea industry had since its inception (Sharma: 2008) encouraged unofficially to sustain the traditional institution of Dhami-Jhakri which was brought about by the workers from their places of origin to heal the workers whenever they used to suffer from sickness of various types. Doing this, the British planters could easily divide the whole working population into various castes and tribes having respective dialects/ languages and thereby continuously maximize their profit margin as no expenditure had to be earmarked for medical facilities of the workers. It was apparently possible for the British planters due to the absence of trade union organizations and collective bargaining for the workers (Bhowmik: 1995). Secondly, each labour Dhura dwellers were encouraged to have its own Bhatti (liquor furnace) where the workers of a particular caste or tribe could drink Rakshi, Jnar(Chiyang) etc.(liquors) made of fermented millet or rice and thereby forget their sorrows and melancholy caused to them by the plantation system (Sharma: 2000) and sleep at night without food being fully drunken. This may be the apparent reason why we still note of the preponderance of tuberculosis caused due to taking only liquors among the plantation workers in the Himalayan tea industry. At that time, the Dhami-Jhakri system urgently needed for the establishment of Bhattis in tea industry to prepare the above liquors as their ritual items to accomplish especially the seance (Chinta) by the Dhami-Jhakris. The isolated nature of the plantation industry along with the day long strenuous work of manual type from the sunrise to sunset throughout the week in the past till seventies of 19th century used to make the workers indentured and lured if not they would be ousted from the plantation system stating them as the disobedient coolies under the Hatta Bahira system. The Hatta Bahira system continued at the plantation industry of the region (Sharma:2008) till the seventies the 19th century. That made the workers sick and they had no modern organizational (industrial) means to cure the patients who used to be suffered from various sorts of diseases. Rather, the plantation system supported, of course, unofficially, for the institutionalization of traditional healing practices through Dhami-Jhakris among the workers (Bhadra: 1997) in the Himalayan tea industry because the planters could not have to spend single pie for the medical treatment of the workers.

The Dhami-Jhakris of Nepali Society

Earlier, the Dhami-Jhakri (Shahmen) as a system of institution was mostly believed to be a hereditary and thus a boy must take the profession of his father as Jhakri as soon his father dies. The workers are of the belief that the Dhami-Jhakris have spirits and demons which are asked to perform various tasks. They are believed to have been helped by the Jhakris to become big sorts within a very short span of time. Such were their earlier beliefs.

Normally, it is a fact that in any tribal community in the world, where modernization has not much influenced the people for their ancient traditions are matter of extreme importance to them and occupy a vital place in their various activities both physical and mental. To cure diseases the Dhami-Jhakris are informed and as they beat their Dhyangro (drum), they expel the evil spirits which have caused the illness. When death occurs in the tribal families, these Dhami-Jhakris beat Dhyangros and make the path for deceased's soul to go into the upper realms of earth or heaven. At the same time, the Dhami-Jhakri who is sedating the process, goes into a trance and during the period, the soul of deceased person is supposed to speak through the mouth of Dhami or Jhankri. The soul of dead person laments and wails but is coaxed by those elder persons present on the occacion by appealing the spirit through Dhami-Jhakri to kindly go to heaven. It is also believed that the Dhami-Jhakris are capable of retarding hail storms, making rain in time and performing such supernatural feats. Conducting Kul Puja (Pitri Puja/Kuldevta Puja etc.) meaning thereby the worship of ancestors, the workers believe that the Dhami-Jhakris act like the bridges between the ancestral spirits and the households. Thus, these Dhami-Jhakris are considered to be the apostles of power (Shakti) and Pita (father). So, every person can not be a Dhami or Jhakri unless he is instructed by gods in his or her dreams or taken by Ban Jhakri (Forest Shahman). Only then he or she can be a Dhami or Jhakri under certain prescribed process of training. The Jhakris or Dhamis wear a white turban having Rudraksha (a kind of holy rosary) and bells, necklace around his or her neck, a Dhyangro(drum) is held on one hand and Gajo (curved stick) to beat the Dhyangro on the other. Seated on a Mandro (woven bamboo mat) or a Gundri (woven straw mat) near Than (alter) and chant his Mantras or Mudhum and supporting Dhyangro on his knee, slowly and with an interesting rhythm. Soon the beat of Dhyangro becomes fully rhythmic, jingling the bells on necklace and rattling the Rudraksha beads. This is strange and exotic to look at as it has hypnotic effect on the spectators in the pregnant silence of surrounding at night. The Dhyangro that is used is made in a ring shape of wooden material on which a skin of an animal is stretched on both sides. There are holes in the edge of wooden material of Dhyangro where various objects are hung. These objects are:- small stars, moon, sun, swords, Khukuris, axes and such numbering about 36 altogether appear to be the decorative ornaments on the Dhyangro. These objects also function along with the shaking of

Dhyangro when the Dhami-Jhakri convulses spasmodically at first and then rhythmically later on.

The real Puja (Chinta) or the seance starts when the Dhami-Jhakri declares that Deota Ayao (sit tremble when the god posses his body) through which he expels the evils spirits within the house and village as a whole. The seance goes on through out the night while the Dhyangro keeps on beating its rhythmic tattoo till next day morning when the seance is over.

During any sickness, the proclivity to immediately estimate the source of the same by the Dhami-Jhakri is found to be common. The Dhami-Jhakri states the reason for sickness to be due to the aggrieved Bhairav or Kul devta, or any other such evil spirit according to the symptom and here the patient family is to make a Vakal (vow) to offer blood sacrifice doing a seance if the sick person is confirmed to be recovered. This is very much prevalent and in a great majority too. Instead of carrying the patient to the hospital, the diagnosis is done by the Dhami-Jhakri who show the cause normally to be due to the evil spirits or Bhut-Pisach, or Bhut-Pret thus requiring the service of Dhami-Jhakri who does Jhar-Phuk or Fa-Foo. The existence of Bhut- Pisach or Bhut-Pret is found to be believed by the workers. The Bhut-Pisch as well as Devta - Devi Pujas take place simultaneously. Still they believed that the deceased souls trouble their families. They also believed on Bhedeko (bewitch). Here, in this context, the Dhami-Jhakri uses the branch of plants with the leaves on it (Shyawlas) and beat on the body of the patient that makes the patient say what the reason is. A diseased soul becomes Masan or great evil spirit if the death ritual is not done properly. Such Masan is also called Jagitra (when a young boy or girl died in accidents or due to untimely death and the Jagitra has not been able to liberalize to go to heaven) meaning thereby an ancestor spirit who has been left behind dangling in between the living being and the dead soul who has not yet attained liberation or Moksha. They also believed that there are Ban Jhakris (forest shahmen who are believed to be wild men and wild women) living in the forests as experts on Shahnism and they look to be less spoken, short in physical appearance and dwarf like.

Concept of Diseases and Employment of Dhami-Jhakris among the Workers

As already mentioned in earlier sections, the Dhami-Jhakri system as a traditional means to cure the diseases, had its origin with healing practices of various tribes and sub-tribes of Nepal and the Eastern Himalayas. The concept of health encompasses two facets, viz, idea regarding diseases and measures for treatment. Since the tea plantation workers are closely associated with their traditions, they still have ample knowledge about the herbal plants to cure the patients (Sharma: 1997). This along with their deep faith and confidence on the secrets of exorcism duly practiced by Dhami-Jhakris, both as a means of healing the patients and source of recreation for them (Macdonald: 1976) became very prominent not only in the past but also today in the plantation industry. By 'disease', they believe the misfortune caused by some supernatural beings or demons who can be pacified by sacrificing animals' blood with the secret Mantras(prayers) chanted by the Dhami-Jhakris(Barreman: 1972). The whole process of doing the seance is called Mudhum especially among the Rai and Limboo castes and Chinta among other castes. However, due to indiscriminate deforestation around the plantation industry during the last few decades, the use of traditional herbal medicines has been decreasing considerably. But the institution of Dhami-Jhakri as a traditional healing system of treatment of diseases is still sustaining well among the workers who are mostly illiterates or semi-literates. Let us see the types of Dhami-Jhakris as we found today in Kaman-Bustees of Darjeeling- Sikkim Himalayas as also in various places of North- East India.

Table 35. Castes/Tribes and Dhami-Jhakris

Sl. No.	*Castes / Tribe*	*Dhami-Jhakri*
1.	Bahun/Chhetri/Thakuri/Kami/ Damai/Sarki (Caste)	Dhami
2.	Newar (Sub-Tribe)	Gubhaju
3.	Sunuwar " "	Puimbo/Ngami
4.	Rai " "	Bijuwa
5.	Limboo (Tribe)	Phedangma
6.	Sherpa " "	Lama
7.	Gurung (Sub-Tribe)	Ghybring/Pajyu/Khepre
8.	Manger " "	Jhakri
9.	Thami " "	Khami
10.	Lepcha (Tribe)	Bumthing/Mun
11.	Bhutia " "	Pow/Nejum
12.	Tamang " "	Bombo/Namisor Jhakri

Source: Sharma: 2005, Gautam and Mangar: 1994.

The table No. 35 indicates that Tagadharis had since time immemorial their own Jhakris popularly known as Dhamis who used to mostly belong to Thakuri, Chhetri, Bahun (Tagadharis) besides a few Kami, Damai and Sarki (untouchables) castes of Nepali society. There were Bahun priests who could not however formally sacrifice animals blood and use wine while doing the rituals to cure the deceased workers instead they used to utter some religious Mantras (prayers-hymns) from Puranas and other Hindu religious scripts and literature. The Bahun/Chhetri Dhamis also used to sacrifice animals blood while doing the seance. With the influx of some Bahuns to Benaras for Sanskrit education since early 19th century, their system of blood sacrifice of the animals started declining. Similarly, Matwalis had their respective Jhakris who used to compulsorily use wine and animals blood in healing the patients. Interestingly, according to a study conducted by Khemraj Sharma, there were only 1129 Tagadhari workers off 52,588 tea plantation workers in Darjeeling hills in 2000 A.D.(Sharma: 2000) which means that there were 51,459 Matwali workers who were believed to have been fully possessed with the Himalayan cults of the past. This may be the reason why the Matwali Jhakris are found in adequate number who use wine and sacrifice animals blood while performing the ritual known as Chinta (seance) which takes place at black nights to liberalize the patients from the clutches of demons. At normal time, if any person falls sick, the Jhakris undertake Jhar-Phuk or Fa-Foo chanting the secret Mantras (prayers) with a few pieces of rice or ginger at their hands and throw the propitiated rice or ginger out to the courtyards duly touching the body of patients. It is known as Sergam. The items so thrown out are consisted of evil spirits and the items so thrown out are called Pansaunu (to push aside at a bypass) and the items are considered as Pansayako which should not be touched by any person. It is also observed that the solutions, suggestions and decisions so taken or sorted out by the Jhakris are final and binding on all the concerned people to get rid of diseases. Due to the existence of Matwali majority as workers in the Himalayan tea industry, the employment of Jhakris is very popular among the Matwalis than Tagadharis. In fact, in the past, some Tagadharis used to do Kul Puja in the form of Masto ritual (Gautam and Mangar:1994) when they used to invite their respective Dhamis (Pradhan:1991). There were mainly two categories of prominence among 12 Mastos gods of the Tagadharis, viz, Pathurnee (possess the Shahman and speak through his body) and Na-Phaturnee (did not possess Shahman and speak through him). The Masto was of Phaturnee and Na-Phaturnee types as they were invisible forces who could be tackled by respective Dhamis. Most of the Tagadharis are educated Babus (clerical staffs) in tea industry of the region although some Tagadhari workers mainly the Chhetris and Thakuris have been found employing the Matwali Jhakris to heal the patients while they do their Kul Pujas at homes by the heads of the families. This is due to the bare fact that

Tagadhari Dhamis are not mostly available at the region today. Whatever the Tagadharis are there as workers in the plantations, they are not much inclined to observe the Masto rituals as in the past due to Matwalisation (Tribalisation) process in the Eastern and North Eastern regions of the country.

The Chinta (Seance)

Both Hinduism and Budhism of the Himalayas have assimilated elements of primitive tribal cults. They are based on the beliefs of supernatural being which always do personification of natural phenomena. There is a belief that certain persons as Jhakris have the ability to communicate with natural phenomena. The Jhakris are noted for trance and spirit possession. The repeated chants made by the Jhakris along with the beating of drum (Dhyangro) as well as drinking Rakshi, Jnar (Chiyang), Nigar etc. made of fermented millet and rice (Pradhan:1991) makes the seance (Chinta) not only healing the patients but it also appears to be the source of entertainment for the spectators. In order to do Kul Puja, marriage and death rituals, each and every caste or tribe must have its own caste/tribal Jhakri. Therefore, every effort is to be made to procure respective caste/tribal Jhakri for such occasions. The Lord Siva is to be first worshipped and then respective Guru (teacher) while doing a seance ritual by the Jhakri. However, for a Dhami, his teacher is one who taught him at home while for a Jhakri, Ban Jhakri is his teacher who taught him at jungle. Falaknu (chanting and trembling the body) along with beating of Dhyangro (drum) rather uttering Mantras (prayers) of religious books is the basic difference between the ways of doing Pujas by the Jhakris and priests (Pandits). The Jhakris put Bhutti (amulet) on the body of deceased person for six month or one year or more as per the instruction of Jhakris. The Bhutti is propitiated at seance ritual. To do a seance ritual, a Mandap (alter) is to be erected with Gungrings (small type of Bamboo) and if it not available around than the normal bamboo can be collected for the same while a Pandit erects Mandap(alter) with banana trees for religious Pujas. However, both the Jhakris and Pandits do consider their respective Mandaps as sacred places. It is known that normally Bokshis (witches) and Chauras or Bokshas (warlocks) act like their enemies in their normal working life or traveling at nights. Coming to question of qualities to be possessed by the Jhakris, it is comprehended that the skill to invite the evil spirits and secondly, the skill to farewell the same are primordial qualifications to be acquired by the Jhakris in order to establish their supremacy over the evil spirits. Yet, quite often, the Jhakris have to celebrate appeasing ceremony for the evil spirits and the ceremonies are known as Siya Marnu (Putla Garnu) by the respective caste/tribal Jhakris. So, only the presence of own caste/tribal Jhakri matters much as he is considered as Sipalu (skilled) Jhakri. But today, any caste/tribal Jhakri is considered for seance provided he is a Shipalu (skiled) Jhakri. This is the area of cultural integration as brought about by the Dhami-Jhakri system in the Nepali society while in the past, only own caste/tribal Jhakris were considered to be employed as skilled Jhankris. To the workers, a skilled Jhakri is one who can easily instructs and gets the evil spirits to do any kind of job as per the discretion of the Jhakri. This is reported by Jhakris that the Sipalu Jhakri instructs the Masans/Bhut-Pisach or Bhut-Pret (evil spirits) to cultivate land at night, destroy the adversaries of his Jagamans (customers) etc. while the Pandits (religious priests) can not directly instruct the good spirits (Devtas) to do so. Considering the influence of modern medical facilities in the region under study, most of the Jhakris feel that with the years gliding by, the institution of Jhakri system and so their knowledge about the herbal medicines and medicinal plants is withering away in modern society of tea industry. It shows that the Jhakri system has not been able to earn much adoration as in the past from the people especially among the present young-educated generations of the region (Sharma: 2003).

Jhakri System: The Emerging Synthesis (Fusion)

Over the last few years due to the wide spread popularity gained through the Annual Jhakri Festival during the Makar Sagranti(15th January) at the confluence of Teesta and Rangeet rivers by Darjeeling Gurkha Hill Council and the Government of Sikkim at Jorethang, South Sikkim, the Jhakris of various castes and tribes of the region have been corporately re-designated as "Gurkha Jhakris". It means that Phedegma, Bijuwa, Bumthing, Lama, Dhami-Jhakri etc. of various castes and tribes of the Nepali society are commonly used by all the tea plantation workers. Interestingly, under the process, the Ojhas who used to be invited in the past from the plain areas by Tagadharis are no more found in significant number. The popularity of Matwali Jhakris is increasing by leaps and bounds in the region due to the overwhelming influence of Matwalisation (Tribalisation) process as a holistic or unifying force or synthesis (fusion) in the plantation industry in particular and Darjeeling-Sikkim Himalayas as well as North Eastern region in general. One of the reasons for increasing popularity of the Tribalisation (Matwalisation) process is due to the fact that so-called Sanskritisation process being popularly lead by the Tagadharis has not been able to bring the dominant Mangoloids (Matwalis and Tribals) of the region in the higher position of caste hierarchy of the Nepali society (Pradhan: 1991) till today. Thus, the Dhami-Jhakri system is still predominant among the Matwalis than Tagadharis to not only heal the diseases of the workers but also to carry out other socio-cultural activities of the society.

The Plantation Universe and Options for Jhakris

Analyzing the data collected from the responses of the workers of Darjeeling hills regarding their options for Jhakris at the time of illness of their family members, following picture has been apparently evolved. This observation can help us to appraise the nature and extent of modern health practices and facilities provided to the plantation workers as per the avowed provisions of Plantation Labour Act, 1951 followed by the West Bengal Plantation Labour Rules (1956) and bipartite and tripartite agreements done from time to time for the workers.

Table 36. Caste/Tribe and Option for Dhami-Jhakri

Sl. No.	*Caste/Tribe*	*First Option*	*Second Option*	*Third Option*
1.	Bahun	Doctor	Dhami (Chhetri, Thakuri/Kami/ Dama/Sarki)	Bijuwa (Rai)
2.	Chhetri	Dhami	Doctor	-do-
3.	Thakuri	-do-	Jhakri	Doctor
4.	Rai	Bijuwa (Rai)	Phedegma (Limboo)	-do-
5.	Limboo	Phedegma	Bijuwa	Dhami
6.	Newar	Gubhaju (Newar)	Doctor	Dhami-Jhakri
7.	Manger	Jhakri (Mangar)	-do-	Bijuwa
8.	Gurung	Ghybring/ Pajyu/Khepre/Lama (Gurung)	Dhami-Jhakri	Doctor
9.	Tamang	Bombo (Tamang)	-do-	-do-
10.	Thami	Khami (Thami)	-do-	-do-
11.	Sherpa	Lama (Sherpa)	-do-	-do-
12.	Lepcha	Bumthing (Lepcha)	-do-	Dhami-Jhakri
13.	Kami	Dhami-Jhakri	Bijuwa	Doctor
14.	Damai	-do-	-do-	-do-
15.	Sarki	-do-	-do-	-do-
16.	Sunuwar	Puimbo/Ngami/ (Sunuwar)	Dhami-Jhakri	-do-
17.	Bhutia	Pow/Nejum (Bhutia)	Ghybring/Pajyu/ Khepre	Khami/Phedegma

Source: Field Work : 2007, Gautam and Thapa Mangar: 1994.

It is very much transparent from the table No. 36 of the study that except Bahun, all other castes and tribes first opt for their respective caste and tribal Jhakris. Even the Chhetri caste opts for Dhami in the first instance as they were traditionally called Matwali Kshetri (Gautam and Thapa-Mangar: 1994). It shows that the Matwalisation (Tribalisation) process has tremendously influenced almost all the Nepali castes and tribes. The Chhetri, Manger, Newar and Lepcha workers also offer their second option for the doctor to heal their patients. But the numerical strength of Newar, Manger, Lepcha and Chhetri castes and tribes is very insignificant having two or three percent of the total workers in the plantations. While Rai is the most dominant caste followed by Tamang caste (now Scheduled tribe) in Darjeeling-Sikkim Himalayas in general and tea plantations in particular. Now, the Limboo caste of the Nepali society also got the status of scheduled tribe in Darjeeling-Sikkim regions. It is also observed from the table No. 36 that almost all the workers of various castes and tribes give their third option to the doctors when their patients become serious (Sharma: 2005). Thus, doctor is the last option for treatment of their patients. Interestingly, it is also found that the treatment of doctor is simulataneously supplemented by observing the religious rites (Pujas) by Pandits (priests). Therefore consulting doctors and inviting the religious priests (Pandits) appear to be the last options for the workers when their patients are left to the wishes of Almighty only.

Role of Jhakris in other Socio-Cultural Activities

The Jhakri system as a social institution is most predominant especially among the Rai, Limboo, Tamang, Newar, Gurung, Manger, Sunuwar, Thami and Lepcha castes/tribes in the industrial society which is the centre of Hindu-Budhist cultural traditions of the region. The tradition is fully exposed even in Mahakal Than (Mahakal

Baba Dham) at Darjeeling - the place where Hinduism and Buddhism of Darjeeling Himalaya have been perfectly synchronised. The Phedegmas and Bijuwas are formally invited from Kalimpong, Mirik, Sikkim and Nepal to conduct marriage and death rituals of Limboo and Rai (Kirantis) families. After the completion of ritual ceremonies by Phedegmas and Bijuwas, the Hindu priests are also invited to do the Hindu religious rites pertaining to marriage qnd death prescriptions. Similarly, Newars invite Gubhajus for the same. Thamis invite the Khamis for the jobs. The Sunuwars invite Puimbo or Ngami, Lepchas invite Bumthings and Gurungs invite Ghybrings/Pajyus/Khepres for the same. The rituals so done by the Jhakris of various castes and tribes are based on Bon religious cults (pre-Budhist form of religion of Tibet and it was borrowed by the Tibetans from Siberia) of Nepal Himalayas and so the workers believe that the Bon religious cults were once upon a time in history adopted by the Nepalis of Nepal and North-East India from Tibet (Pradhan: 1991) which was then known as Bhoot or the country of Bhutias. The followers of Bon religion were known as Bonpas. However, it is found that the present generations of workers hardly know about the Bon religion.

Masto: The Tribal God of the Himalayas

The Masto was another popular God among the people of Nepal Himalayas. Studying the Masto, we see its origin with the Aryans who came from Central Asia to Iran, Iraq, Afganisthan, Pakistan, Kashmir (Khasmir) during the first century before Christ. In Central Asia, the Khas are still called "Kas" (Tagadharis of today) had habitation in the river Dangala between Iran and Iraq and the place was known as Khusisthan. It is known that prior to 12th century A.D., there was Khas empire of Non-Vaidik Aryans. The Non-Vaidik Aryans as we found in Mahabharat were Khas. The Khas empire was in Karnali zone of Western Nepal. In many instances of the Nepali history, there is a mention of Khas Desh and Khas Kura (language). The Khas people used to worship cow and land. Along with cow and land, the Khas people used to worship Masto (Kuldevta) and Bhawani goddess. The Bhawani goddess are called Vidyabhasini. Thus, Bhawani and Masto were the creation of Khas people of the Himalayas. For Khas people, Vayu god is the greatest god associated with Masto. The Vayu (evil spirits) were to be made Kul Devtas by observing a seance by the Dhamis. The Vayus were evil spirits due to untimely death of a family member caused by accident or suicide. The Vayu is also called Jagitra among the Tagadhari Khas people of the Himalayas. This may be the reason why still in some remote villages of the Himalayas where Bahun-Chhetris are in majority are called Vayu Gaons or the villages of Vayu Jats. They have belived to have Vayu Dhamis. It is also believed that Masto became popular after the fall of Khas empire in Karnali zone in Western Nepal. With the increasing influence of Sanskritisation process under Hinduism and Buddhism in Nepal, the Masto worship became indiopensable among the Khas Tagadharis. In some stray writings in Nepal, the literature on Masto rituals among Tagadharis have been referred to have been found in the Himalayas ever since 1365 A.D. In 1617, King Gaganiraj has mentioned that he got Janai (sacred threads) by way of doing Masto ritual. In 1833. A.D., king Rajpita Jaisi has mentioned Kul Devta-Masto and Nine Bhawani goddesses in his hand written document known as Graha Santi-Bibaha Padatti. With their emigration from Karnali zone to other parts of Nepal Himalayas, they inherited Masto-Kuldevata and nine Bhawanis. Although we have heard about 12 Mastos, there were in fact altogether 36 Mastos in different places of the Himalayas. Each clan of a caste among the Tagadharis had its own specific Masto. The 36 Mastos of the Khas people were as follows:-

(1) Dadar Masto, (2) Rumal Masto, (3) Dare Masto (4) Dude Masto, (5) Khaper Masto, (6) Kala Sila Masto, (7) Vavira Masto, (8) Vami Masto, (9) Bura Masto, (10) Tharpa Masto, (11) Kawa Masto, (12) Vas Masto, (13) Laukuri Masto, (14) Riwmi Masto, (15) Sim Masto, (16) Kurmi Masto, (17)

Rumal Masto, (18) Dadisital Masto, (19) Latto Masto, (20) Chetrapal Masto, (21) Vuro Masto, (22) Garuli Masto, (23) Vetpal Masto, (24) Puwalo Masto, (25) Tuesepani Masto, (26) Vabira Masto, (27) Tero Masto, (28) Muruli Masto, (29) Mandali Masto, (30) Rud Masto, (31) Keilo Masto, (32) Devithan Masto, (33) Sundor Gar Masto, (34) Chal Masto, (35) Tare Masto and (36) Kalo Masto.

It was found that there were no similarity between Nau Bhawani of Khas people and goddess Durga of the Indian Hindus. This is because of the fact that Nau Bhawanis are totally called by the different names, viz, Vidyavashini, Chungalni, Kalika, Vandali, Dingekni, Purungalni, Keshwalini and Jalapa. Worship of Masto and Nau Bhawani is simultaneously done by the Khas people of the Himalayas. There is no specific form or image for Masto gods. The Masto is worshipped in a holy place at home called Gar Bhandar after cleaning the same with cow dung. However, in some places especially jungles, Kul Devta Dhamis or Jhakris made the images of Masto with mud and this mud image along with Trishul, Bell, Sankha, Diyo, Kalas etc. are made is used as the means to worship the god, Masto, Although the Masto is worshipped as a kind of spirit or Vayu god among the Tagadhari Khas people of Nepali society, it epitomised a rich cultural heritage of the people of Himalayas as a whole.

From the above discussion, it revealed the fact that all the 36 Mastos were not simultaneously worshipped at a time by a caste in a particular place. But the names and types of Masto might have increased with intensity of migration of the Khas people from Western to Eastern Nepal Himalayas and further to East and North Eastern Indian Himalayas.

Masto: The Forgotten God

Literally, by now, we are able to understand by "Masto", the Khas people of Himalayas (Bahun, Chhetri and Thakuri) used to believe as their "Kuldevata". It is also explained by some scholars mainaly in Nepal and Sikkim that prior to

1306. A.D., Masto, the son of Lord Indra came down to Dadar (Western Nepal) from Kashmir (Khas-mir) Himalaya and met nine Durgas there and adopted them as his nine sisters. Over the period of time, the form and type of Masto went on increasing from one place to another from Western Nepal and spread over to other parts of Nepal and further to Indian Himalayas. In each region, different name has been given for the Masto. Take for instance, in Jumla (Western Nepal), the name of Masto was known as Babiro, Buda, Tharpa, Kava etc. The Masto is also found to be worshipped by Garwal Hindus. However, in the beginning, Masto was popular among Bahuns, Chhetris and Thakuris as well as among the Kamis in Western Nepal. To worship each Masto, respective Dhami was a Must. So, to worship various Mastos, people had to employ different Masto Dhamis. This is evident from the table No. 37 of the study.

Table 37. Name of Masto and Associated Caste of Dhami

Sl. No.	*Name of Masto*	*Caste Associated with Dhami-Jhakri*
1.	Buda Masto (Western Nepal)	Chhetrti
2.	Bhatpal Masto „ „	Kami
3.	Khaper Masto „ „	Thakuri
4.	Tharpa Masto „ „	Chhetri
5.	Kala Sila Masto „ „	Chhetri
6.	Dara Masto (Ukali/Orali) „ „	Brahmans
7.	Dud Sila Masto „ „	Thakuris
8.	Chetrapal Masto „ „	Chhetris

Source: Macdonald: 1976; Field Works: 2007.

In fact, there were 12 Mastos in the beginning as twelve brothers. But among the twelve Mastos, only 08 Mastos became very prominent later on as they used to protect the men from evil spirits, dishonest persons, enemies and Tibetan infiltration in Western Nepal Himalayas. It indicates that the Masto as an ancestral god had neither came from

Tibet nor from the Indian plains. However, in the beginning, Sanyasis of Nepali community had no Masto. As stated above, each Masto had to have respective Dhami. A person could become a Dhami when god climbed on him which was locally called Deota Autriyako (god climbes on the body of Dhami). Such Dhami was to be known as Kul (Masto) Dhami. They used to believe to have both village and family Mastos. The Mastos were believed to left a family or place if they are not properly worshipped. The Dhamis were considered as the keystones for Masto rituals because they were chosen by the gods for such appropriate jobs. Therefore, unlike priesthood, the institution of Dhami was not at all always hereditary. Thus, a Dhami did not have been trained by any other Dhami or Jhakri. The sign of his calling was trance. The most striking feature of a Dhami was to have a long tuft of hair (Latta). Such a long tuft of hair was also found among the Jagaris of Jagarias of North-West provinces of India adjoining Nepal at that time. The long hair was called Jhaakro but it was not related with Jhankris of Magars of Central Nepal. It was because of the fact that unlike Jhankris, Dhamis did not use drum (Dhyangro) as Hindu Khas of Western Nepal did not use the musical instruments made of the flesh of animals. Only the untouchable castes used to handle the musical instruments in Western Nepal at that time.

Each Dhami of respective Masto used to have his distinct type of rhythms (Gai). The institution of Dhami was omnipotent element in Masto temples of villages. The Bahuns and Dhamis together used to worship Masto and at the end of worship of a particular Masto, all other twelve Mastos were also to be given offering by the Bahun priests. The Bahun priests also used to participate in Dhami seance (Chinta) in full moon nights.

Corporately, there were two types of Masto, viz, Dhudha Masto or Dudha Sila Masto who were to be offered Kheer

(Loose rice dish made of rice, milk, sugar and other spices) and Dara Masto or Kala Sila Masto with long teeth was to be offered the blood and flesh of gentle animals like He-goat, pigeon etc. The Mastos of Bahuns, Chhetris and Thakuris used to be offered the blood and flesh of young He-goats to Dare Mastos who were also known as Phaturnee Mastos while Dhudh Sila Mastos were known as Na-Phaturnee Mastos. The He-goats were considered as gentle animals which could even be eaten by Bahuns, Chhetris and Thakuris. While the Mastos of lower castes like Kami, Damai and Sarki used to offer blood of impure animals (for pure Hindus) like pigs, bufallows, fowls etc. In most parts of the Western Nepal villages, Masto temples or Kotgaris were errected as the temples for village Mastos and therefore, Masto ceremony was common to all the people living in the villages. While in Eastern Nepal and Indian Himalayan niches, the institution of Masto is rather an individual concern and is worshipped as Kul Devta among the Khas (Tagadhari) people of the regions.

Mastos were not truely gods but the protectors of gods or Kul Devatas. Therefore, it was believed by all that if gods were aggrieved, then some misfortunes would be taken place among the families or persons of the families. Such misfortunes were to be promptly reported to Bahuns (Pandits) who would suggest the concerned persons to consult their respective Kul Dhamis. Thus, a kind of triangular relationship was believed to be on vogue among Bahun, Dhami and Masto. In this way, Mastos were considered as the rectifiers for evil doers in the society. Unlike Jhakris, the Dhamis of respective Masto (12 Mastos) did not observe Guru Puja in formal way. For Dhamis who were associated with Mastos, the Lord Siva used to be considered as their Guru because the Mastos were believed to be masculine genders. It may be the reason why there were 12 Mastos and 12 Mahalingams pertaining to Lord Siva.

With the amalgamation of Khas people with other Nepali castes, the institution of Dhami is being renamed giving generic term as Dhami-Jhakris without any distinction in day today life. However, among the Khas people of Darjeeling-Sikkim Himalayas, Masto Dhamis are still prevalent in places like Sikkim, Darjeeling, Kalimpong, Mirik, Bijanbari etc. and North-East India although the Masto rituals are done at the individual Khas households. Among the Bahuns, Chhetris and Thakuris, the "Goth Dhup" for Ukali and Orali gods is still done in the cow sheds of the people in the month of Mangsir (December) and Vaisak (March) every year. Among the Bahuns, Bhattarai and Dhakal clans for instance, of Terai area of Nepal, Kalimpong, Darjeeling, Sikkim and other North Eastern regions of the country, the Mastos are very popular. Even the youngsters also know or have heard about the Kul Devtas though they are not well informed about the Mastos as the original forms of Kul Devatas. By "Kul Devtas", at least, they know little about the "Forefathers" who are taken as the symbol of respect and veneration.Another view is that the family members who died in accidents or suicides become Vayu (Jagitras) who are to be made Kul Devta (family god) with the process of Siya Marnu by Dhamis and such Kul Devatas are to be pleased in every ritual ceremony as done by the Bahun priests in the house of Tagadharis even today. Thus, the Masto as forgotten god is the issue to be addressed seriously by the Anthropologists.

Tradition Vs. Modernity

The garden society is basically a tradition bound society. Whereever any person of the family falls sick, they consult Dhami-Jhakri (Shahmen) first and undergone seance. The moment patients become serious, they rush to hospitals or doctors for treatment. It is found that except Tagadharis, all the Matwalis prefer Dhami-Jhakri first and at the flag end, the patient is sent to the hospital. Even during the treatment of patient at the hospital, religious rituals, are done at home with the suggestion of Dhami-Jhakris. The various health provisions as enshrined in the Plantation Labour Act, 1951 have hardly able to convince the workers so far about efficacy of modern health practices in the plantations. This is due to the tribal background of the plantation workers. In fact, tribalism as a way of life has tremendously affected the health dimensions of plantation workers in North-East India.

9

Summary and Conclusion

(I)

Change is the law of nature and men being part of it also change in their socio-economic set up which is brought about by their immediate environment. The post-nineties era of the 19th century as well as early twenteeth century brought about a drastic change in our economic life due to Liberalisation, Privatisation and Globalization of our national economy. Tea being part and parcel of Indian economy has also been influenced by the process of globalization. What appears in tea front is the question of survival and it is possible through adopting competitive culutre by leaving the traditional style of functioning.

Historically speaking, the emergence of tea industry was the result of British process of globalization with reference to country like India. At first, tea was introduced in Assam. The British government started exploring the Darjeeling hills, Dooars and Terai belts of West Bengal and got complete success. Thus, by 1840 tea was introduced in Darjeeling hills, in 1874 at Dooars and Terai in 1864. In South India also tea industry was started around fifties of eighteenth centruy.

The growth of tea industry was very fast in the initial stage of its introduction till 1947. After the independence of the country, the number of plantation started declining especially from 1951 to 1962 due to the fall of tea prices and internal distrubances in the country. However, there were 744 tea plantations in Assm in 1961 and the number increassed to 750 in 1971. The number of tea garden further increased to 850 in 1991 and now the same number of gardens have been reported in Assam.

Similarly, in West Begnal, there were 301 tea plantations in 1961 and it increased to 305 in 1981. In 1996, the number of plantation increased to 374. Besides West Bengal and Assam, there were 2,563 tea gardens in North India (except Assam and West Begnal) in 1981 and reached to 2,948 in 1996. Tamil Nadu, Karnataka and Kerala are also tea growing regions of India. But what is to be noted is that there the size of gardens is small compared to Assam and West Bengal. There were 9,498 tea gardens in South India in 1971 and number increased to 10,937 in 1981 and in 1996, the number of Indian tea garden further increased to 13,936. Today, there are about 14000 tea gardens in India.

With the increase in number of gardens, the area under tea also correspondingly increased over the four decades. In 1961, there was 16, 2367 hectares of land under tea in Assam. The hectarage under tea reached to 23,4580 hectares in 1996. In West Bengal, there were 82,705 heactares of land under tea in 1961 and it increased to 100,650 hectares in 1996. In other tea gardens of North India (except Assam and West Bengal), there were 256928 hectares of land under tea in 1961 and it reached to 345988 hectares in 1996. Similarly, there was 74,301 hectare of land under tea in South India in 1981 and it reached to 76,125 hectares in 1996. Thus, in all India, altogether there were 331229 hectares of land under tea in 1961 and the same increased to 421913 hectares in 1996.

The enhancement of hectare to 421913 under tea was possible due to enhancement of various developmental programmes of tea plantation relating to extension, replacement and replanting activities. It is observed that in 1961, a total of 1713.47 hectares were extended, 352,77 hectares of land were replanted by new plantations and 1781.87 hectares of land were replanished in India. In 1971, the area under extension reached to 2355.35 hectares with 201.12 hectares under replanting and 1118.96 hectares under replacement progarammes. In 1981, a total of 1986.50 hectares under extension, 475.75 hectares under replacement, 1288.98 hectares under replanting programmes were done in India. Similarly, in 1981, a total of 2423.05 hectares under replacement, and 1446.48 hectares under replanting were brought under the tea cultivation. On the average, a total of 2543.25 hectares under extension, 379.28 hectares under replacement and 1389.53 hectares of land under replanting were done to produce more and more tea in India.

With the increase of tea plantation and areas under tea cultivation, tea production scenario also underwent considerable increase in India. For instance, at the national level, it is seen that a total of 639864 thousand kilograms of tea was produced in 1984 and the production increased to 780 million kilograms in 1996. Interestingly enough, it is observed that inspite of increase in areas and number of gardens, the yield rate was not very perceptible and uniform. For instance, the yield rate in 1984 was 1606 kilograms per hectare per year while the rate of yield came down to 1523 kilograms per hectare per year in 1986. Again, in 1993, the yield rate further increased to 1819 kilograms per hectare per year. While the yield rate decreased in 1994 to 1768 kilograms per hectare per year and in 1996, it was 1797 kilograms per hectare per year. It was expected to raise to 3000 kilograms per hectare in 2000 A.D. if proper care was done in the context of three to four years as we had the capacity to produce another 485 million kilograms of tea in 1996-97-98. These 485 million kilograms of tea in addition to earlier production could be grown as we had 24,1631 hectares of land laying vacant inside the plantations. Again, we had 7031 hectares of land as fallow land in the plantations, 16811 hectares of land available for extension, 16,972 hectares of land laying unutilised in government vested land and 16,050 hectares of land was available in the degraded forest areas of the government.

If these lands were properly utilised then we would be able to produce about 1111 million kilograms of tea by 2000 A.D. of which 824 million kilograms would be available for domestic consumpltion and 287 million kilograms would be available for global markets as exportable surplus.

These observations can be supplemented by the fact that alomost 10.0% of land in tea plantations are given to manpower resources to cultivate vegetables throughout the year. Unfortunately, these lands more or less remain barren throughout the year due to the non-availability of adequate water, manure etc. to cultivate the land. So, it is suggested that instead of cultivating vegetables in the land, tea may be grown which proves to be more profitable and productive to the manpower resources. In Darjeeling, there are 90,000 acres vacant land which can be utilised for the cultivation employing one lakh workers.

Another important aspect relating to the necessity of improving production is to change the company policies, relating to replacement, extensions and replanting programmes in their tea estates. If this is not done then sooner or later foreign tea might capture completely the national tea market also as it is mostly happening in case of Indian tea in global tea markets especially by Srilanka and Kenya. Very recently, Nepal Tea has also getting good hold in Indian market that has caused tremendous challenges to Darjeeling Orthodox tea in the national markets.

(II)

One of the important development of Indian tea industry is the emergence and growth of small growers tea plantations since 1989. The small grower gardens means the tea gardens having 8.09 hectares to 50 hectares of land under tea plantations without having processing or manufacturing factories (units). There were about 300 such small tea gardens in North Bengal and now in 2008, there are more than ten thousands small grower gardens in West Bengal, 30,000 in Assam and another ten thousands in South

India. The North India produces 10000 lakhs kilograms of green leaves and in South more than 2,290 lakhs green leaves were producing in 1996. Therefore contribution of these small grower gardens have been coupled with certain unique problems. The green leaves have to sell to the bought leaf factories where they do not get good prices. Only Rs.7/- per kilogram of green leaves is given. Secondly, they have got the problem of acquiring NO OBJECTION CERTIFICATE from the government due to politics of the ruling government in West Bengal. They do not have specific financial institution to finance them in appropriate time and also they do not get technical expertise services to assist them in this venture. If these problems are overcome specially in North Bengal there will be every scope of its increase in near future.

(III)

Among the various factors of production, worker is very important in the agro-based industry. The tea plantation workers in India are immigrants or descendents of immigrants from various parts of the country.The characterisitc features of the plantation workers are their heterogeneous features cut across by caste and tribal (ethnic) background. For all practical purposes, the low wages, coercion and indenture are the nature of recruitement, administration and work organisation in tea and other plantations of North-East India.However, ever since 1947 with the emergence of trade union movement in the plantations, the system of cellective bargaining had been given little relief to the workers.

Being labour-intensive industry of the country, the number of tea workers have been increased to 11 lakhs today. Every seventh worker of organised sector workers of the country is a plantation worker. For instance, there were 9,48,598 workers in 1950 in the country and number increased to 9,86,781 in 1990 in India. Only during 1961 to 1971, the number of workers came down to 7,66,593 due to the Indo-Chinese and Indo-Pak wars and Bangladesh war of liberation.

The number of tea garden workers had been further increased due to the introduction of small tea grower gardens and new plantations in India. For instance, there were about fifteen thousand workers in small grower gardens in 1996 in North Bengal and 10,760 workers in Assam and about 5,000 workers in South India in 1996. The number had increased to fifty thousands in 2007. But with the beginning of 2008, the number of tea garden workers has tremendously decreased due to contratualisation or casualisation in tea industry of the country.

Interestingly, it is also observed from the study that the tea plantation workers are low paid compared to other organised sector workers of the country as tea workers are regulated by Minimum Wages Act, 1948 through tripartite agreements. Among the tea growing states, Assam and West Bengal have low rate of wage than South India. The wage rate is Rs. 58.00 today in West Bengal plantations per day per worker while in Assam it is Rs. 62.00 per worker per day.

The plantation workers are protected of course theoretically today by various labour acts as these acts are also on vogue in the period of globalization. In this respect, Plantation Labour Act, 1951, Maternity Benefit Act,1961, Equal Remuneration Act, 1976, Payment of Wages Act, 1936, Employees Provident Fund Act, 1952, Industrial Employment Standing Orders Act, 1946, Payment of Bonus Act, 1972, Payment of Gratuity Act, 1965, Trade Union Act, 1926, Minimum wages Act, 1948, Industrial Disputes Act, 1947 etc., are applicable to the workers. Besides these acts, concerned state governments make their own labour rules relating to these acts suitable to their plantation situation.

(IV)

It is apparent from the study that tea industry is human resource intensive industry and therefore their research and development is indispensable which is possible through training and education. In the recent years, keeping this in view in tact, certain research institutes have come up to train managers of the plantations. The Indian Institute of Plantation Management, Bengalore, Tea Research Associations, UPASI, Tea Research Institute, Assam - Agricultural University, Tea Board of India, National Institute of Plantation Management, Siliguri, Tea Research Centres etc. have emerged in the country. But these institutes confer trainings to the managers only and thus very often whole lot of plantation workers are devoid of the facilities.

In order to bridge the gap, the Government of India through Central Board for Workers Education under the Ministry of Labour and Employment had launched the workers education scheme in the country ever since 1958. The Board conducts various types of training programmes for the workers of organised, unorganised and rural sectors of our economy. In the initial stage, board used to educate the organised sector workers on trade unionism. But with the change of the national industrial environment, the training programmes also underwent a drastic change towards productivity education to quality and cost effectiveness education today through joint educational programmes in organised sectors and awareness programmes in unorganised/rural sectors. For tea plantation and other plantation workers, the Board conducts trainings on productivity, Quality, Cost Effectiveness and cost reduction education to have bright future of the plantation industries of the country in general and North-East India in particular.

(V)

In order to have bright future, certain planning is needed everywhere and therefore in tea plantation industry also. To attain this, the planning for small growers and new plantations seems to be very important relating to issue like replanting, infilling of vacent land in tea estates, rejuvenation purning, irrigation, soil conservation, cultural practices, factory capacity, flooded situation of the plantations of Assam and West Bengal, plucking techniques, organic tea farming system etc. are to be done immediately. Of course, doing these works initially plantations have to incur substantial amount of money but after five years it can harvest good crops for years together. This will enable us to have a self-sustained productivity and growth in tea industry which will be able to meet domestic as well as foreign markets.

The progress of tea industry will not only encourage the national economy but also the fate of 11 lakhs workers and their dependents of the plantations and outside. The workers have therefore to think to reorient their work culture. The mamagement has also to reorient their approach from tradition to modernity in order to bring a new work culture in tea industry of the country in the real sense of the term both for today and tomorrow.

(VI)

Today, in the transitional period of globalization, keeping abeyance the provisions of Indian labour legislations is the best option ever articulated by the globalization of Indian economy on tea frontiers. These days, it is observed that in most of the plantations of the region, hardly the workers get their rations except once or twice in a month. No house repairing work has been done since the last one decade or so. Regarding medical incentives, the same tablets are given for headache, fever, stomache etc. Coming to the question of wage issue, now (2008) the workers are paid various types of wages for work pertaining to different rounds of plucking of tea such as:-

(i) Rs. 58.00 for 6 days round;

(ii) Rs. 52.00 for 7 days round;

(iii) Rs. 50.00 for 8 days round;

(iv) Rs. 48.00 for 9 days round;

This is a kind of pro-rata system beings administered by tea management for the payment of wages of the workers. The same calculation is being done in case of Bonus,

Gratuity, Provident Fund, medical facilities, rations, maternity benefits and other incentives of the workers. The Doubli (extra leaf prices) to the tune of actual round of plucking is the new criteria followed today for extra leaf payment in high plucking season. It means that if a worker plucks extra tea leaves on 6 days round then she or he is entitled for the highest rate of Doubli payment. The extra leaf price for plucking is therefore varies from 6 days to 9 days rounds in the plantations. The rate of extra leaves plucked also varies from one plantation to another.

This is done to increase the labour productivity keeping in view of having the quality tea leaves. Such a pro-rata system has been fastly extending to each and every aspect of the plantation industry today. It indicates the obvious reason for the deduction of all sorts of facilities to the workers. To pluck tea leaves on rotation (plucking rounds) depends on the decisions of the management and not the workers.

Here in this respect, gevernment is simply articulating one whimsical alternative to another without implementing none in full for the tea plantation workers. This is the main reason why productivity of labour is decreasing considerably because of wrong decisions of tea garden management and government. Secondly, doing this, number of Hazira workers are leaving the plantations and plantation jobs for ever and it has however provided complete liberty to the tea garden management to employ as much Thicka (casual) workers as possible especially in high plucking season. Thirdly, the tea garden management do not have to bother about the principle of labour standards in the form of Dastur (convention) to do and as per the provisions of Indian labour acts and local situation most of which including the Plantation Labour Act, 1951 are voluntary in nature and implication. Fourthly, trade union leaders of the plantations have accepted the introduction of pro-rata system as they are able to get labour contracts from the tea garden management. It indicates the nature of establishment of strong management-labour union nexus in tea industry of the region. Finally, there is absolutely the end of working class identity in tea industry.

(VII)

The tea plantation workers of the North-East India and region under study appear to be hardly the subject to be incorporated in the labour policy of government. The garden workers are at times misguided either by the management or trade unions or government agencies and also other agencies of the society. Talking about the socio-economic conditions of tea plantation workers, it is found to be perfectly not uniform as it varies from one plantation to another. It again varies from one company to another due to their specific company industrial philosophy. The government mechanisms keep mum till any serious problem crops up at the garden giving simply vague justifications. Today, just to somehow manage tea gardens is the basic short cut philosophy of all partners of tea industry of the country.

(VIII)

No one either from trade unions or management or the rank and file workers of the plantations happens to be transparent about the conditions of the plantation workers through different medias. The "Enclave Tea Economy" is dealt with very rarely by some outside urban based medias with biased interpretations that hardly reflects the genuine agonies of the workers in the period of globalization since every body from medias is also busy having given importance to income security rather than job security. This is the main reason why mainstreams being unknown to their genuine identity often call them immigrants or the descendents of immigrants. It is because of this fact, the Gurkha National Liberation Front (GNLF), the local political party of Darjeeling for example, did not at all bother about the closure of tea gardens in Darjeeling hills. Rather GNLF preferred for the closure of tea gardens which to GNLF could at least enable the tea plantation workers to own their permanent homes and land for their graveyards. This would give workers the specific addresses that could rather reflect the restoration of their ethnic identity in Darjeeling hills in truest sense of the term.

(IX)

To a have a tea garden for a person (of course to a trader) in Darjeeling hills is meant to acquire lot of schemes from the Tea Board of India with handsome subsidies and also to have name and fame or honor before the Indian Chamber of Commerce and Industries and also to have name to the Commerce and Industries Ministry of Government of India. Again, it is also found that very many tea owners feel it a pleasure and status sybmol in the national mainstream to have tea gardens in Darjeeling hills.

(X)

It is therefore visualised from the study that the days will definitely come by 2020 A.D., when alomst all the plantation workers will consist of female and female workers only because the tea garden males do not at all prefer the tea garden jobs in the globalized era. Thus, feminisation process under the globalization policy shall have complete hold on tea industry of Darjeeling hills by 2020 A.D.

(XI)

Therefore, it is also visualised from the study that globalization may be successful to establish only two classes, viz, rich and poor by 2020 A.D. because the very fundamentals of working class concept having middle class layer will definitely vanish from the Indian industries including the tea industry of the region. It will be a kind of purely agrarian society under the global evolution process which has had undergone its dynamics from agriculture to industrial to technological and it will be going back to the complete agrarian formation by 2020. A.D.

(XII)

Ever since the introduction of tea industry as "Enclave Economy" of the British government, it could not end its colonial characteristics in so far as its modus operandi is concerned. Under the influence of globalization, policy, having purely technological evolution, the human resource of the industry has also become as good as a technical commodity. Thus, once again, the tea plantation workers are being treated as the cheapest commodity to be purchased and sold (hire and fire or fight or flight) under the forces of globalization of tea plantation frontiers of North-East India including the Darjeeling hills.

(XIII)

Sociology of work in regard to tea garden Hazira system has been drastically altered. Earlier till 2007, the Hazira consists of the total leaves plucked including the Black (big) leaves which after sorting out could be separated and be thrown out at the factory itself and hence the workers could get Hazira on the total tea plucked. But after January, 2008, the black tea leaves are to be plucked and be separated at the field only and such black tea leaves do not come under consideration of the total tea leaves plucked in course of weighing the same. Thus, the workers have to bear double losses in regard to plucking the leaves on the one hand and they are getting less weges on the other. This has resulted into the escalation to the plucking tea leaves by the regular 'permanent' workers especially the male workers. That may be one of the apparent reasons why labour productivity is decreasing day by day and the regular workers are leaving the tea garden jobs because they can not fulfill the targeted Hazira and thereby expected wages. In the situation, the management on the other hand are very happy to employ the casual (Thiccka) workers who are seasonal workers having no deep commitments and dedication to the tea industry of the region as no extra facilities except the wages are paid to the workers. It may be the reason why today even in Dooars areas of West Bengal, more than 60.0% of tea plantation workers of plucker category are females and only 10.0% to 15.0% of males are real tea plantation workers of plucker category because the remaining 25.0% males are either factory workers or office staffs or supervisory sub-staffs while in Darjeeling only 15.0% to 20.0% males are factory workers or supervisory sub-staffs and office staffs and thus hardly 10.0% of the workers are male tea plantation workers of plucker category. Hence, the feminisation process as brought about by the globalization has mostly affected the labour intensive agro-based tea industry of the region.

The globalization has also affected the workers work structure and payment of wages. In some gardens, workers are paid only five days wages for doing six days work. The number of bungalow staffs has also been drastically reduced to the minimum resulting which the good many experienced managers are leaving the gardens for elsewhere the country and abroad to acquire their proper professional status.

Another spectacular change that has taken place among the workers is that the garden Samajs (social organisations) are asking their worker members to send their children outside the gardens keeping in view of the uncertainty of tea industry in near future. This has tremendously affected the tea industry because of the paucity of male workers. Even the job related to chemical fertilisers and pesticides to be pasted at the tea bushes are to be get done by the female workers of the plantations. These jobs however come under the purview of hazardous jobs not to be get done by the female and child workers. This has affected the health aspect of the female and child workers in tea plantations during the recent era.

It is also found that during the last one decade, the plantation management of the region have started recruiting female supervisory sub-staffs keeping in view of the increasing female work force in the plantations. Many tea garden owners have also started to employ female Assistant Managers in their plantations so as to tackle the female work force of the gardens accordingly.

(XIV)

With the influx of traders in tea plantation industry, of Darjeeling hills, alomst all the labour standards except wages have been curtailed down drastically Except six tea plantations under the Gooderick Tea Groups and one under Duncan group (corporate houses), the remaining 63 gardens of Darjeeling hills are under the proprietary companies today. They have asked the government to either relinguish them from paying any other facilities to the workers as per the provisions of labour legislations of government except wages or ask the workers to run the industry by themselves through Self Help Groups or Workers Cooperatives. The trade union leaders are happy to have been run the industry by the workers through cooperatives or through Self Help Groups because they can earn money as they themselves purchased the green tea leaves at lower cost than the amount they get from the gardens where they supply the green tea leaves being purchased from such cooperatives or self help groups. The vehicles to carry the green tea leaves to the established gardens are also owned by the these contractors (trade union leaders) and thus they earned good money from their vehicles also. This is apparent from the case of Pashok and Via-Tukvar tea estates of Darjeeling hills which were somehow run by such contractors during their closure period (16 years) since early nineties to 2006. A.D.

(XV)

The role of government to the Himalayan tea industry is hundered percent indifferent especially taking the issue about the cause of the working class of the plantations. Whatever the steps being taken by the trader owners of the plantations in the globalized era, they are accepted blatantly by the government since the government is interested merely with the revenue and revenue only from the tea gardens and their owners and thus government has nothing to do about the socio-economic development of the workers. The management pay Rs. 20,000/- to the tea garden panchayat annually. In most of the cases, the money again goes to the hands of the trade union leaders as contractors cum panchayat members who have in most of the cases hardly utilize the same for developmental works in the plantations. This is apparent from the road conditions, houses, hospitals, water facility, fuel facility etc. of the present day tea garden workers. The contractors-management nexus is so concretised that the contractors have constructed cemented houses in the plantations while the workers huts have hardly been repaired since the last one decade or so. This may be the reason why the tea garden workers told us that to them whether the tea industry sustains or not makes no difference to them as they feel that tea industry of the region is good as an old fort. The fort is being desolate whether due to the soldiers are eaten by the tiger or they fall off the cliff. Thus, the morale and morality of the workers have been at very low ebb today in the globalized era. Merely giving them the whimsical assurances from the various corners of the society can hardly bring back their lost morality and morale into proactiveness today in so far as their socio-economic agonies are concerned.

(XVI)

Talking about the bush productivity through replantation by replenshing the old bushes, most management people of the industry stated that the present clones planted in Darjeeling gardens do not have the Darjeeling type of flavour which the old bushes have retained since over hundred and seventy years. It is because of the fact that they can not just do anything except to sustain the Darjeeling flavour to attract the international buyers. The cost of production of Darjeeling tea varies from Rs. 350/- per kilogram to Rs. 500/- per kilogram while in 2007, they got the price on the average at Rs. 250/- only per kilogram. This has further cracked down the industry due to the demand for hundered percent bio-organic tea by the Darjeeling foreign buyers because the cost of production has been increased considerably over the last two decades.

(XVII)

The fall outs of the globalization have been viewed beautifully on Making Globalization Work by Joseph E. Stiglitz (2007) to the world of labour. Stiglitz found that developed countries like U.S.A., Germany, U.K., France, Italy etc. wanted to pass stringent international laws which can be forcefully imposed on the developing countries by way of bribing the politicians and government so as to do crimes on the poors. The international trade as conducted between the developed and developing countries is perfectly on unequal terms. Doing this, the labour front has become almost dumping stock as they have left behind on mobile in search of just marginal jobs of unskilled types. This is more rampant in case of agrarian related workers of the world. The idea that Stiglitz has expressed in his book have hundered percent repercussion in the plantation frontiers of the nation considering the mushrooming of the vested interest groups into one conglomeration. This is apparent from the denial of incorporating the international labour standards for Indian workers by the national government. So, the impression expressed by the plantation workers that they have nothing to do with the issue like Globalization in so far as their socio-economic development is conerned may be correct to a great extent in the plantation frontiers of North-East India including the Darjeeling hills.

(XVIII)

The "Vision 2020" for North-East India of the gevernment has nothing to do with the plantations and plantation workers in so far as their improvement is concerned. The whole gamut of development strategy under the vision is centered around the tribal development and agrarian development to achieve self-reliance through capacity building. The strategy is conerned mostly in a few states of the region only. The plantation industry is rather subsidiary to the people at large due to its colonial nature of production relations. In fact, even the government has ordained colonial status to the industry and is trying to liberalise from the age old slavery by suggesting the workers to manage the gardens through their cooperatives or self help groups.

(XIX)

The emergence of ideal tea industry in the region is expected only with the influx of industrialists or corporate houses on tea in the truest sense of the term. Otherwise the demise of tea industry is highly expected vision by 2020 A.D. In this venture, government should come forward to laison the corporate houses and multinational companies at least to sustain the industry beyond 2020 A.D. The whole history of tea industry needs to be rewritten with denovo outlooks from concerned partners of the industry. The blemishness as prevalent work culture of the industry does not however no more reap any meaningful outcome for the sustenance of the industry for long. Unlike other professionals, workers as human resources of the industry also want income security rather than job security today. The workers wage was to be revised from 01.04.08 but so far no step is being taken by the concerned tripartite organisation (Kolkata) which is known as Consultative Committe of Plantation Associations, to sit in time and settle for the wage revision, although tea garden management of the region have already started pro-rata system by which almost all the welfare incentives have been made redundent or curtailed drastically or made conditional (Wage-Productivity Nexus) today.

Bibliography

Asopa, V.N. : (2004), Competitiveness in Global Tea Trade, Oxford University Press and IBH Publishing House, New Delhi.

Assam Tea Review : (Dec. 2007), Vol. 96, Kolkata.

.... : (Jan., 2007), Vol. 16, No. 11, Kolkata.

Barrreman, G.D. : (1972), Hindus of Himalayas; Ethnography and Change, University of California, Berkeley.

Bhadra, Mita : (1992) Women Workers of Tea Plantations in India, Heritage Publishers, New Delhi.

Bhadra, R.K. : (1997. Social Dimension of Health of Tea Plantation Workers, N.L. Publishers, Siliguri, West Bengal.

.... : (1997), Plantation Labours of North-East India, N.L. Publishers, Dibrugarh (Assam).

Bose, Ronnie : (2007), Survival of the Fittest in Assam Tea Review, Dec. 2007, Vol. 96, No.10, Kolkata.

Bhowmik, Sharit : (1981), Class Formation in the Plantation System, People's Publishing House, Delhi.

.... : (1995), Tea Plantations in West Bengal in Sarath Davala (Ed.) Employment and Unionisation in Indian Industry, Friederick Ebert Stiftung, New Delhi.

.... : (1996), Tea Plantation Labour in India, Friederick Ebert Stiftung, New Delhi.

.... : (2008), Productivity and Labour Standards in Tea Plantation Sector in India, Tea Despatch, West Bengal (Siliguri).

CCPA : Consultative Committee of Plantation Associations, Tea Industry : A Report, 1996, Kolkata.

Dash, A.J. : (1947), Bengal District Gazetteers (Darjeeling), Government Printing Press, Alipur, Calcutta.

Deb, Tapan Kumar : (September, 2007), Tea Despatch, Siliguri (W.B.).

Devi, Uma : (1989), Plantation Economy in Third World, Vikas Publishing House, New Delhi.

Gautam, R. & Thapa Mangar, Ashoke : (1994), Tribal Ethnography of Nepal (in two Vols.) Book Faith India, New Delhi.

Gooptu, Nandini : (2007), "Economic Liberalisation, Work and Democracy" in Economic and Political Weekly. May, 26-1 June, Vol. VIII, No. 21, Mubmai.

Government of India : Plantation Labour Act, 1951, Industrial Disputes Act, 1947, Employees Provident Fund Act, 1952, Payment of Gratuity Act, 1972, Payment of Bonus Act, 1965, Maternity Benefit Act, 1961, Equal Remuneration Act, 1976, New Delhi.

Government of West Bengal : (1956), Plantation Labour Rules, Alipur Government Printing House, Calcutta.

Government of Assam : (1956), Plantation Labour Rules, Guwahati.

Government of Tripura (1956), Plantation Labour Rules, Agartala.

Greaves, I.C. : (1957), "Plantation in World Economy" in Eric Wolf (Ed.) Plantation System in New World. Washington Pan American.

Griffith, P. : (1967), The History of Indian Tea Industry, Weidenfel and Nicholson, London.

Hunter, W.W. : (1876), A Statistical Account of Bengal, Concept Publishing Company, Delhi.

ILO : (1950), International Labour Organisation : Basic Problems of Plantation Workers, Geneva.

Jones, W.O. : (1968), "Plantation" in David L. Sills (Ed.) International Encyclopaedia of Social Seience, Vol. 8, Macmilan Press, New York.

Kar, R.K. (1981), Savaras of Mancotta, Cosmos Publications, New Delhi.

Lama, M.P. and Sarkar, R.L.: (1986), Tea Plantation Workers in the Eastern Himalayas, Atmaram and Sons Publications, New Delhi.

Macdonal, A.W. : (1976), "Preliminary Report on Some Jhamkri of Munglan" in John T. Hitchock (Ed.) Spirit Possession in the Nepal Himalayas, Vikas Publishing House, New Delhi.

Mukherjee,S. : (1987), "Dooars Plantation Economy : Evolution and Pattern of Change" in R.K. Bhadra (Et.al. Ed.) Plantation Labours of North-East India, Siliguri and Dibrugargh (Assam).

Munch, Ronaldo : (2002), Globalization and Labour : The New Great Transformation, Madhyam Books, Delhi.

Myint, Hla : (1973), Economics of Developing Countries, Hutchinson University Press, London.

Northey, W.B. & Morris C.J. : (1976), The Gurkhas : Their Manners, Customs and Country, Cosmo Publications, New Delhi

O'Malley, I.S.S. : (1947), Bengal District Gazetteers "Darjeeling" Logos Press, New Delhi.

Pathak, Avijit : (2006), Modernity, Globalization and Identity : Towards a Reflexive Quest, AAKAR BOOKS, DELHI.

Pradhan, Kumar : (1991), The Gurkha Conquests, Oxford Univeristy Press, Calcutta.

Ratnam, Venkata, C.S. : (2001), Globalization and Labour Management Relations : Dynamics of Change, Response Books, New Delhi.

Rubber Board of India : (2007), A Diary, Ministry of Commerce and Industries, Government of India, Delhi.

Sharma, Khemraj : (1994), Socio-Economic life of Cinchona Plantation Workers in Hill Darjeeling, Thesis approved by University of North Bengal, Darjeeling, West Bengal for the award of Ph.D. (Arts) degree.

.... : (1997), Socio-Economic life of Cinchona Plantation Workers in India, N.L. publishers, Dibrugarh (Assam).

Sharma, Khemraj : (1999), Tea Industry in India : An Introduction, N.L. Publishers, Siliguri, W.B.

.... : (2000), The Himalayan Tea Plantation Workers, N.L. Publishers, Dibrugargh, (Assam).

.... : (2003), Tea Plantation Workers in a Himalayan Region, Mittal Publications, New Delhi.

.... : (2005), Sociology of Indian Tea Industry, Mittal Publications, New Delhi.

.... : (1997), "Trade Union Movement in Cinchaona Plantation Industry in Hill Darjeeling" in R.K. Bhadra (Et.al.Ed.) Plantation Labours of North-East India, N.L. Publishers, Dibrugargh, (Assam)

Sharma, K.R. & Das, T.C. : (2005) "Quality Environment of Tea Plantation Workers : A Study in North-East India" in S.K. Ghosh and V. Parmeswaran (Ed.) proceedings of 4th Indian Congress of Central Board for Workers Education, New Delhi, published by the Oxford Publishing Company, University of Jadavpur, Kolkata.

.... : (2008), Agony of Plantation Workers in North-East India, Kalpaz Publications, New Delhi.

Stiglitz, Joseph, E. : (2007), Making Globalization Work, Alan Lane, London.

Subramaniam, Bala : (1995), Tea in India, Publication and Information Directorate, New Delhi.

Tea Board of India : (2007 and 2008), Tea Statistics and Tea Digest (1996), Ministry of Commerce and Industires, Govt. of India, Kolkata.

Verma, M.P. : (2008), Salvation of Abandoned Closed Tea Gardens, Assam Tea Review, 26th January, 2008, Vol. 96, No. 11, Kolkata, West Bengal.

Wolf, Eric : (1959), "Specific Aspects of the Plantation System in the New World" in Eric Wolf (Ed.) The Plantation System of the New World, University of Washington Press.

Xaxa, V.: (1997), Economic Dualism and Structure of Class, Cosmo Publications, New Delhi.

Index

O

P

Q

R

S